Destination
MULTIMEDIA

by Aaron E. Walsh

IDG Books Worldwide, Inc.
An International Data Group Company

Foster City, CA ♦ Chicago, IL ♦ Indianapolis, IN ♦ Braintree, MA ♦ Dallas, TX

Destination MULTIMEDIA

Published by
IDG Books Worldwide, Inc.
An International Data Group Company
919 E. Hillsdale Blvd., Suite 400
Foster City, CA 94404

Library of Congress Catalog Card No.: 95-77671

ISBN: 1-56884-470-0

Printed in the United States of America

10 9 8 7 6 5 4 3 2 1

1E/RY/QZ/ZV

Distributed in the United States by IDG Books Worldwide, Inc.

Distributed by Macmillan Canada for Canada; by Computer and Technical Books for the Caribbean Basin; by Contemporanea de Ediciones for Venezuela; by Distribuidora Cuspide for Argentina; by CITEC for Brazil; by Ediciones ZETA S.C.R. Ltda. for Peru; by Editorial Limusa SA for Mexico; by Transworld Publishers Limited in the United Kingdom and Europe; by Al-Maiman Publishers & Distributors for Saudi Arabia; by Simron Pty. Ltd. for South Africa; by IDG Communications (HK) Ltd. for Hong Kong; by Toppan Company Ltd. for Japan; by Addison Wesley Publishing Company for Korea; by Longman Singapore Publishers Ltd. for Singapore, Malaysia, Thailand, and Indonesia; by Unalis Corporation for Taiwan; by WS Computer Publishing Company, Inc. for the Philippines; by WoodsLane Pty. Ltd. for Australia; by WoodsLane Enterprises Ltd. for New Zealand.

For general information on IDG Books Worldwide's books in the U.S., please call our Consumer Customer Service department at 800-762-2974. For reseller information, including discounts and premium sales, please call our Reseller Customer Service department at 800-434-3422.

For information on where to purchase IDG Books Worldwide's books outside the U.S., contact IDG Books Worldwide at 415-655-3021 or fax 415-655-3295.

For information on translations, contact Marc Jeffrey Mikulich, Director, Foreign & Subsidiary Rights, at IDG Books Worldwide, 415-655-3018 or fax 415-655-3295.

For sales inquiries and special prices for bulk quantities, write to the address above or call IDG Books Worldwide at 415-655-3200.

For information on using IDG Books Worldwide's books in the classroom, or ordering examination copies, contact Jim Kelly at 800-434-2086.

For authorization to photocopy items for corporate, personal, or educational use, please contact Copyright Clearance Center, 222 Rosewood Drive, Danvers, MA 01923, or fax 508-750-4470.

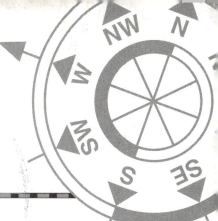

full motion

The quality of playback for a computerized movie or scene. A full-motion movie will play smoothly, without skipping frames or jumping and jerking about. Although a movie or portion of a multimedia title may proclaim *full-motion video* capabilities, this does not automatically mean your computer will play it smoothly. Full-motion video is recorded with all of the individual frames necessary to produce smooth play, but it requires a lot of computing horsepower to achieve the desired effect. If your computer system isn't up to the challenge, a full-motion video will seem choppy as your computer struggles to keep up with it.

the Internet

A vast, globally connected computer network developed by the United States government after World War II. Although originally designed to provide scientists and researchers with the ability to communicate using computers, the Internet has grown rapidly over the past decade to include a diverse group of approximately 30 million users worldwide. Internet content is as diverse as it is vast, with nearly all modern documents, correspondence, and software products available for the taking.

Microsoft Video For Windows

Also known as Audio Video Interleaved (AVI), Microsoft Video For Windows is similar in nature to Apple's QuickTime. Full-motion video capabilities are provided without the need for specialized hardware using this technology. Audio is interleaved with video to provide smooth, synchronized playback of both media.

full screen

Images and video residing on computers can be viewed in a variety of sizes, and larger sizes require more computing power. QuickTime and Microsoft Video For Windows typically record and play back at small sizes, although it is also possible to record and view at sizes as large as the computer monitor itself. Full screen refers to an image or video that is as large as the monitor, and significant computing power is required for smooth playback.

MIDI (Musical Instrument Digital Interface)

A specialized music technology, typically a combination of specialized hardware and software, that provides the ability to record and/or play back musical instruments using the computer. MIDI music is very different from computerized digital audio sources: Digital audio is an actual recording of music, whereas MIDI is similar to sheet music that is used to command different musical instruments, which, when played together, generate the final audio sound.

About the Author

Aaron E. Walsh

Aaron E. Walsh is President and CEO of Mantis Development Corporation, a Boston-based software development firm specializing in graphics technology. Formerly a consultant for Boston College's Advanced Technology Group, he has more than 15 years of experience designing state-of-the-art software products. Aaron has written several articles for leading software journals like *MacTech Magazine* (formerly *MacTutor*) and *Dr. Dobb's Programming Journal.*

ABOUT IDG BOOKS WORLDWIDE

Welcome to the world of IDG Books Worldwide.

IDG Books Worldwide, Inc., is a subsidiary of International Data Group, the world's largest publisher of computer-related information and the leading global provider of information services on information technology. IDG was founded more than 25 years ago and now employs more than 7,500 people worldwide. IDG publishes more than 235 computer publications in 67 countries (see listing below). More than 60 million people read one or more IDG publications each month.

Launched in 1990, IDG Books Worldwide is today the #1 publisher of best-selling computer books in the United States. We are proud to have received 8 awards from the Computer Press Association in recognition of editorial excellence, and our best-selling ...For Dummies™ series has more than 17 million copies in print with translations in 25 languages. IDG Books Worldwide, through a recent joint venture with IDG's Hi-Tech Beijing, became the first U.S. publisher to publish a computer book in the People's Republic of China. In record time, IDG Books Worldwide has become the first choice for millions of readers around the world who want to learn how to better manage their businesses.

Our mission is simple: Every IDG and Compaq Press book is designed to bring extra value and skill-building instructions to the reader. Our books are written by experts who understand and care about our readers. The knowledge base of our editorial staff comes from years of experience in publishing, education, and journalism — experience which we use to produce books for the '90s. In short, we care about books, so we attract the best people. We devote special attention to details such as audience, interior design, use of icons, and illustrations. And because we use an efficient process of authoring, editing, and desktop publishing our books electronically, we can spend more time ensuring superior content and spend less time on the technicalities of making books.

You can count on our commitment to deliver high-quality books at competitive prices on topics consumers want to read about. At IDG Books Worldwide, we value quality, and we have been delivering quality for more than 25 years. You'll find no better book on a subject than an IDG book.

John J. Kilcullen

John Kilcullen
President and CEO
IDG Books Worldwide, Inc.

Dedication

Dedicated to my family, with love, who taught me early on that faith the size of a mustard seed can move mountains. And to Basia, without whom this book wouldn't have been possible, and with whom all mountains become molehills.

Acknowledgments

With thanks to the original nucleus of Mantis Development Corporation, whose own faith and continued support over the years have formed the backbone of this company. In particular I'd like to thank Talbott Crowell, Ed Greene, Don Higgins, Jeff Lynch, Robert Wade, and our Board of Directors.

The fine folks at IDG Books Worldwide, especially Eric Stone, the publisher of this book; Pradeepa Siva, the marketing muscle behind it and the person through whom I was introduced to IDG and this project; and Amy Marks, the editor of this book, whose keen eye and even hand brought much needed temperament to my often unruly prose. Also, thanks to David Vining, Patricia Dalheim, and Pat Kubick at Compaq. Special thanks to Pat Kubick for arranging the Compaq Presario loaner for this book.

My friend Vinnie Falcone, of Apple Computer, Inc.; thanks for all your help, particularly in resisting the temptation to play "Repo-man." The loaner equipment is now ready to return home.

Special thanks to Dr. Gary P. Kearney, champion of Mantis Development Corporation and friend, whose continual support and enthusiasm are a source of great inspiration. And to all my friends at LUA; thanks for everything.

Finally a note of sincere gratitude to my esteemed colleague Barbara J. Mikolajczak, whose considerable efforts and dedication to this publication and to Mantis have easily equaled my own.

(The Publisher would like to give special thanks to Patrick J. McGovern, without whom this book would not have been possible.)

Credits

V.P. and Group Publisher
Brenda McLaughlin

Associate Publisher
Eric Stone

Brand Manager
Pradeepa Siva

Associate Developmental Editor
Amy Marks

Production Director
Beth Jenkins

Supervisor of Project Coordination
Cindy L. Phipps

Supervisor of Page Layout
Kathie S. Schnorr

Pre-Press Coordinator
Steve Peake

Associate Pre-Press Coordinator
Tony Augsburger

Media/Archive Coordinator
Paul Belcastro

Copy Editor
Carolyn Welch

Assistant Editor
Heather Albright

Technical Reviewer
Mark Hall

Project Coordinator
Valery Bourke

Production Staff
Shelley Lea
Gina Scott
Carla C. Radzikinas
Patricia R. Reynolds
Melissa D. Buddendeck
Leslie Popplewell
Dwight Ramsey
Robert Springer
Theresa Sánchez-Baker
Maridee V. Ennis
Drew R. Moore
Anna Rohrer

Proofreader
Phil Worthington

Indexer
Steve Rath

Cover Design
Three 8 Creative Group

Book Design and Layout
Jo Payton

Illustrators
Accent Technical Communications

Screen Captures Used in this Book

Throughout this book, you will see dozens of *screen captures* used to illustrate the potential of multimedia. These screen captures were provided by the vendors listed below. All brand names and product names used in this book are trademarks, registered trademarks, or trade names of their respective holders.

- Adobe Systems

- America Online

- Brøderbund

- CompuServe

- Creative Multimedia

- Electronic Arts

- Living Books

- Macromedia

- Mantis Development Corporation

- MECC (Oregon Trail II, The Yukon Trail, The Amazon Trail, Troggle Trouble Math, and Storybook Weaver Deluxe are copyrights, trademarks, or registered trademarks owned by MECC. Used with permission. All rights reserved.)

- Microsoft Corporation

- Netscape (Netscape and Netscape Navigator are trademarks of Netscape Communications Corporation.)

- Origin

- Prodigy

Table of Contents

Part 4: Getting Multimedia to Work _____ 99

Part 5: Who Is Creating Multimedia? _____ 125

Part 6: Getting into Multimedia _____ 147

Introduction

I'll Meet You on the Other Side

What you are about to enter is a world unlike any you've known before. Stepping into a new era, we are pioneers in an expansion not westward, but inward. Whereas once we lived in an industrial age, today we find ourselves swept into a world revolving not around the physical, but the intellectual and the ephemeral: the information age.

Increasingly we are a society reliant on technology and information. Computers are shifting quickly from yesterday's research tool to today's consumer appliance. Just as the microwave oven, television, and refrigerator have become fixtures in nearly every home across the nation, so too will the computer. And with multimedia, we will use our computers to learn, play, and work in ways our ancestors could not have dreamed.

Brought forth in an industry notorious for its fast pace and constant evolution, the life cycle of the book you are about to read is a perfect example of technology working at its best and with great efficiency. Not constrained by time, space, or location, *Destination MULTIMEDIA* was built entirely using modern technology and in a fraction of the time it would have taken only a handful of years ago. Made possible by the globally connected Internet, laptop computers, and a team of dedicated professionals spread across the continent, this movable feast was as exhilarating as it was challenging.

Written and assembled out of thin air using laptop and desktop computers, *Destination MULTIMEDIA* has grown from concept to reality in less than three months. Written during day-long stints at the Trident Cafe in Boston, on crowded subway trains at rush hour, at the spacious and rejuvenating Sparhawk resort in Ogunquit, Maine, while rocketing across the continent at 30,000 feet in a jetliner, and finally completed amid the tranquility and beauty of a secluded cabin snuggled in the heart of the breathtaking Colorado Rockies, *Destination MULTIMEDIA* was my constant companion during its genesis.

After each part of *Destination MULTIMEDIA* was written, with the touch of a button I transported it across the country to editor Amy Marks using the Internet. Within minutes she had the work in hand and began editing it on her own computer. When done, she forwarded it to another part of the country for technical review. The work then returned to me over the ether and directly into my laptop computer, ready for another round of refinements. A nationwide relay team, we operated in concert as the book took shape, handing off our work to one another as it became ready. Built using the same technology it discusses, *Destination MULTIMEDIA* is a product of the information age.

Product screen images and illustrations for the book were transported by fax, Internet, and overnight courier, orchestrated by Barbara J. Mikolajczak in the Mantis offices in Boston. Cover design and marketing was tackled by Pradeepa Siva, on the opposite coast, again using the Internet and fax technology to keep the work flowing. Our team was in touch daily, relaying files and ideas instantly without so much as a face-to-face meeting or telephone call. What was once impossible was utterly essential to the safe birth and coherent development of what you now hold in your hands.

Multimedia is the most dazzling and beautiful gem in the crown of the emerging information age. I hope you have as much fun learning about this exciting technology as I have using it, and I look forward to hearing from you as we step into this new and exhilarating world together.

Aaron@mantiscorp.com

(Transmitted over the Internet on Sunday, June 11, 1995 at 4:53 p.m. Mountain Standard Time from a cabin somewhere in the Colorado Rockies.)

PART 1

What Does Multimedia Mean?

Unless you've been living underground for the past year, chances are you've heard about multimedia. From television commercials to block buster movies on the big screen to personal computers, multimedia has exploded on the scene and is about to change the way you learn, work, and play. From Times Square to *Time* magazine, a revolution in technology is brewing, and multimedia is heading the charge. At least that's what those of us above ground have been hearing lately, and it's high time you got involved.

What Is Multimedia?

So what is *multimedia?* That's a good question, with a variety of good and not-so-good answers depending on whom you ask. If you were to go strictly by Noah Webster's definition of the word, multimedia would be anything that contains more than one type of medium. A medium is a system or channel of communication or information. Standard media include video, photography, animation, sound, and text. By strict definition, then, television would be the most obvious form of multimedia. After all, television contains two media: video and sound.

▶ *Although television is perfectly capable of displaying multimedia presentations, as often seen in commercial advertisements, it lacks the ability to provide interaction. And without interaction, you cannot truly experience multimedia.*

Does that mean you have been enjoying multimedia from the comfort of your living room sofa all along? Not quite. While it's true that television is indeed a form of multimedia by strict definition of the word, it isn't exactly what most people familiar with the technology would call *true* multimedia. In fact, it would probably be a good idea to refrain from referring to your TV as a multimedia device in public lest you enjoy being thought of as the neighborhood oddball.

Although debate continues over what constitutes true multimedia, one thing is certain: television, as we know it today, isn't multimedia. It is merely a device on which we can watch multimedia presentations that we cannot participate in, such as computer-generated special effects or flashy advertisements. And as we'll soon see, true multimedia is something to participate in, not just to watch.

Conventional wisdom defines multimedia as any combination of images, sound, or text residing on a computer, usually assembled to present information in a form better absorbed by the subject than are traditional formats such as books, magazines, radio, and television. And who is the subject? You are. I am. We all are.

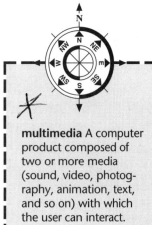

multimedia A computer product composed of two or more media (sound, video, photography, animation, text, and so on) with which the user can interact.

Anyone who uses a computer that has a mouse, anyone who stops at an information kiosk in the shopping mall, and anyone who plays Sega or Nintendo video games is a subject. You may not feel like a subject, but you are. And a good one, I might add. You've been exposed to multimedia in varying degrees for years and haven't so much as flinched. Multimedia is just about everywhere you look today, with the best yet to come. Given this widespread use of multimedia, why haven't you recognized it before? Perhaps because it has crept quietly and swiftly into our everyday lives like morning glories in a garden; by the time you realize its presence, you've already succumbed to its beauty.

This book is intended to help you break away from the passive role as subject. In time, you will understand and utilize multimedia technology in a way that best fits your needs and lifestyle. Empowered with the information you are about to read, you will become an active participant in the multimedia revolution.

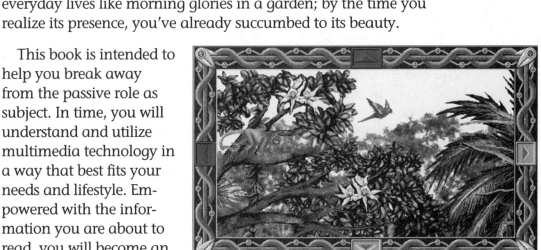

▶ *Multimedia brings a whole new world to your computer.* (*from MECC's* Amazon Trail)

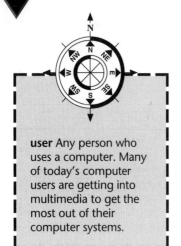

user Any person who uses a computer. Many of today's computer users are getting into multimedia to get the most out of their computer systems.

In the computer industry, you will be known as a *user*. This transition is not difficult and only requires that you understand what has already been going on around you. Let's begin by getting to know what multimedia is and how to identify it.

Count the Media

The best way to identify a multimedia product is to count the media involved. Forms of media include, but are not limited to, motion video, photography, animation, sound, and text. Adhering to the original definition of multimedia, one could argue that the presence of two or more media constitutes multimedia. Practically speaking, however, the presence of multiple media alone does not guarantee a multimedia experience.

Such is the case with television. True, two media are present in TV. But more important than the presence of the media itself is the fact that television audio and video sources are preprogrammed and out of our control; we simply sit down and tune in. Short of channel surfing with the remote, we have absolutely no control of the images and sound coming down the pipe. Although those who subscribe to a pay-per-view service certainly have better control over what they view than those of us who are hopelessly ground into the couch by *Baywatch* and *Court TV,* once the decision is made to watch a television program (pay-per-view or otherwise) we are then bombarded by a predefined sequence of images and sounds. Control of the sequence in which the media is presented is completely out of our hands; the most we can do is change the station or mute the audio portion of a broadcast.

How about the venerable VCR? With this marvel of modern technology we can fast forward and rewind to any part of a video. And that's not all — we can pause at any point, freezing a single frame into place for our viewing pleasure. Here we have more than one media, and what seems to be control over the sequence in which it is viewed. Surely this must be multimedia! But it is not.

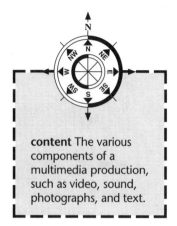

To be considered a true multimedia product by today's standards, a product must provide some degree of control over its *content,* beyond search, play, and pause. Even laserdisc players, with their ability to jump to any section of a movie at any time, are not able to provide a true multimedia experience. Television, VCR, and laserdisc devices are fundamentally the same: You can view the information supplied via cable, video tape, or laserdisc, yet have no real control

content The various components of a multimedia production, such as video, sound, photographs, and text.

▶ *Although a fully equipped home television setup, complete with a VCR and set of giant speakers, may be impressive when it comes to presenting the multimedia commonly used in commercials and special effects, it still fails as a true multimedia device. Even though these multimedia presentations look and sound terrific, the ability to interact with them is missing.*

▶ *Most multimedia presentations products include draw and paint capabilities, allowing those creating the presentation to touch up existing images or create original artwork from scratch.*

over the content. Sure, you can rewind, fast forward, and pause till your thumbs are numb and your eyes are red, but you have absolutely no interaction with the product short of simply moving about the prerecorded content. And without interactivity there is no multimedia, regardless of how many types of media you can count.

While accurately identifying multimedia begins with counting the media itself, a few more pieces to the puzzle must be in place before a product can be classified as multimedia. For the most part, modern multimedia products share the following characteristics:

1. Two or more media are present: sound, video, photography, animation, text, and so on.

2. The user can interact with, or have control over, the product's media.

3. The product resides on, or was created with, a computer or similar device using computation power.

If the product in question possesses these three characteristics, it's a good bet you're looking at multimedia. And although the focus may not be on multimedia itself, chances are the underlying foundation is based on some form of multimedia technology. For instance, the weather maps displayed in many evening news television broadcasts often contain both text and animation and are created using sophisticated computer systems. In addition, a forecaster controls the appearance of each map and its various elements using a hand-held remote. Here we have all the characteristics of multimedia. However, we don't tune in to see the multimedia portion of the newscast. We simply watch the weather report, which happens to have been created using one form of multimedia technology.

The body of work, or production, presents the weather in a form we can best understand. The production in this case could properly be called a *multimedia presentation,* something you watch but do not participate in. It would be incorrect, however, to refer to this production as a *multimedia product.* The term multimedia product refers to something you can purchase or otherwise obtain for the express purpose of using in a multimedia capacity. Television, VCR, and laserdisc technology are all capable of displaying multimedia presentations, although they are not considered multimedia products. These devices are perfectly capable of displaying a multimedia presentation, but they lack the key ingredient of true multimedia: interactivity.

multimedia presentation A multimedia work you watch but do not participate in.

multimedia product Something you can purchase or otherwise obtain for the express purpose of using in a multimedia capacity.

Interactivity

The word *multimedia* first surfaced in the 1960s and seemed to lay dormant until technology revolutionized the concept. In its original incarnation, multimedia meant anything that combined different types of media, such as sound, video, photographs, text, and so on. In short, if multiple media were present, multimedia was an appropriate classification. But, alas, the times they are a-changing. Ice cream has gone from chocolate, vanilla, and strawberry to Chunky Monkey, New York Super

▶ You can use the World Wide Web to play interactive multimedia games with people around the globe.

interactivity The ability to navigate the contents of a multimedia product, giving you some degree of control over it. With an interactive product, you are in control, telling the product where you want to be, what you want to see, and how you want to experience it. If it's not interactive, it's not true multimedia by today's standards.

Fudge Ripple, and Cherry Garcia. *The Brady Bunch* has given way to *Power Rangers.* And multimedia has come a long way, baby.

Enter the age of *interactivity* — the world of modern multimedia. Every thirteen-year-old knows exactly what it is, how to get it, and how to control it. Keep your eye on the teenager who plays Mortal Kombat with religious fervor — he's plugged into multimedia and won't let go short of a power outage. Today's multimedia is interactive, to the point where the terms multimedia and interactive are nearly synonymous. You are in control, telling the products where you want to be, what you want to see, and how you want to experience it. If it's not interactive, it's not true multimedia by today's standards. Just ask your resident Nintendo junky.

Using a mouse, joystick, paddle, touch-sensitive monitor, or data gloves, you become a part of the experience. No longer relegated to the sidelines as a spectator, you are a full participant. Direct the movie instead of simply watching it. Soar through the solar system instead of staring up at the sky. Plunge into the depths of the ocean rather than wade in the shallows. You are versatile, capable, and strong. You become one with the experience, having been sucked wholly into the

▶ *Some of the world's best reference materials are now available in one convenient multimedia product. These products can put at your fingertips a library of reference books, magazines, journals, newspapers, and other sources of information.*

infinite vortex of interactive multimedia. You're no passenger, friend, you're the pilot.

Yeah, right. While multimedia does offer more control than was previously possible with any other media presentation tools, the concept of total immersion, becoming "one" with the product, isn't a reality quite yet. Beware of the hype; it's everywhere you find multimedia. Many manufacturers produce slick, visually compelling packaging and thrill-a-minute product descriptions to sell their multimedia offerings, much of which only vaguely resembles the actual product. The truth is, we've just begun to see the first generation of true multimedia products hit the market. Some are great and some lukewarm, while others aren't worth the cardboard they're packaged in. In all cases, however, true modern multimedia products offer some degree of interactivity. You have control over some aspect of the product, although the kind of control and exactly how much you are given varies from product to product.

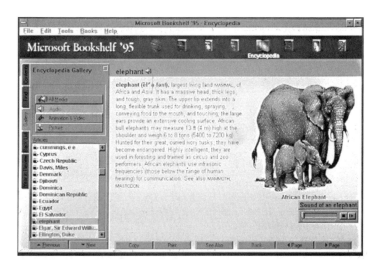

▶ Reference products, such as Microsoft Bookshelf, *let you look up information about a particular subject, in this case, elephants. You can read about them, look at pictures, and even listen to typical elephant sounds.*

Interactivity requires computational capabilities, although not necessarily in the form of a desktop computer as you might expect. Today, even kitchen appliances harness computational power: the ability to compute or calculate. Have you ever wondered how your timer-based coffee pot is able to turn itself on in the morning, brew a perfect pot of java, and then turn itself off exactly on schedule before you've managed to slap the snooze button on your clock

home entertainment systems Small, relatively inexpensive devices that attach to a television and provide entertainment primarily in the form of video games. Extremely popular among teenagers, Atari, Nintendo, and Sega are the most common home entertainment systems in use today.

radio? And just how does that snooze button allow you to catch a few extra winks, when only a few decades ago we had to manually wind up our clocks just to get them through the night?

It all comes down to computational capability, an ingenious combination of electricity and computer chips. How it works might as well be magic, but the end result is nothing short of a modern-day miracle. Over time we have become dependent on the conveniences afforded us by computational power, from automobile cruise controls to time-saving microwave ovens. And over time we will become dependent on multimedia.

However, if the ability to compute were not possible in such appliances, we would have nothing more remarkable than television. Someone other than you would decide what you see and hear, what happens, and in what sequence. But thanks to the computer chip, you are able to control the action. If interactivity is the key to true multimedia, then surely computational power is the metal from which multimedia is forged.

▶ *A multimedia title like* Microsoft Complete Baseball *lets you check a seating diagram for your favorite team's stadium.*

Although desktop computers are the most obvious form of computational power, don't forget that *home entertainment systems* such as Nintendo, Sega, and Atari also contain computer chips and are equally capable of providing multimedia, in many cases better than desktop computers. All multimedia devices, be they computers, entertainment systems, or even information kiosks, enable the user to interact with a multimedia production. All multimedia productions, however, are not created equal.

In its simplest form, interactivity allows you to navigate the contents of a multimedia product in a free-form manner, not restricted to a particular direction or series of events. For example, you are not forced to view the contents in a linear beginning-to-end fashion, as is the case with a television show. Instead, you can jump around to any part of the production at will.

▶ *Your favorite sport takes on a new look when viewed as a multimedia title. (from Electronic Arts'* PGA Tour Golf 96)

Suppose for a moment that you are viewing an interactive multimedia movie. You begin by watching the opening scene as usual. But you soon become bored. Happily, your options are many: leap ahead to see the action or hop around various scenes to find your favorite characters. Read director's notes in text format whenever you want or hear the director talk about the struggles and sacrifices of producing an epic. Listen to the actors describe their favorite parts of the production at your leisure. Experience the movie on your terms; watch the scenes you like when you like and in any order that strikes your fancy. With interactivity, you navigate the contents of a multimedia production by controlling the sequence and manner in which the contents are presented. No longer bound to rigid, predefined productions, you are liberated by interactivity.

At its very best, interactivity gives you the controls altogether. With fully interactive products you become part of the experience, be it a game, advertisement, or homework assignment. Rather than simply navigating the contents as a tourist, you become a central character in the production, seeing and hearing things through the point of view of your character. Fully interactive products are often called virtual reality, although they are not yet realistic enough to be confused with everyday reality. They are, however, incredible examples of multimedia at its best given the current limitations of today's technology. And the field is constantly widening, with new and creative interactive multimedia titles hitting the retail shelves every day. It won't be long before concept and technology converge, permitting full immersion in interactive multimedia productions. The fun is just beginning. Step forward, sit down, and buckle up; it's going to be a fast, bumpy, and exhilarating ride.

Degrees of Multimedia

As you now know, multimedia comes in different forms, from basic content navigation to fully interactive immersion products that place you inside the production itself. The form, or degree, of a multimedia production is dictated by the level of interaction provided, which is closely related to its contents. Products whose content is primarily informational, such as kiosk systems, digital encyclopedias, reference guides, and the like, generally provide the least amount of interactivity and are therefore considered to be the lowest form or degree of multimedia. At the opposite end of the spectrum, the highest degree of multimedia, lie products designed from the onset to offer a full multimedia experience rather than simply provide informational navigation tools. And somewhere in between lies

▶ *With multimedia, you'll be able to go places you never dreamed possible. (from Brøderbund's* Where in the USA is Carmen Sandiego?)

the majority of modern multimedia titles; while not purely informational, these productions don't attempt to provide fully interactive experiences either. Because there are no clear definitions of the various degrees of multimedia available today, it is often difficult for the consumer to judge a product solely on its packaging.

It is important to realize that content alone does not dictate the degree of a multimedia production. Many elements, all of which must be carefully balanced, go into the creation of a multimedia product and ultimately influence the degree of interactivity a product will provide. A single multimedia title typically requires the combined skill of many individuals during the development process, where production budgets and technological expertise often impact the final product to a far greater extent than the content itself. Although excellent content does not guarantee an excellent multimedia title, it's a good start.

Ideally, multimedia productions are built around their content. This is not always the case, however. Oftentimes, content is available while other critical resources are

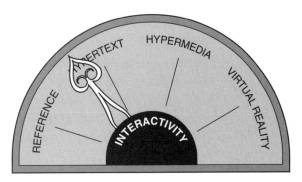

▶ *True multimedia products provide some degree, or level, of interactivity. The simplest degree of multimedia, hypertext, is commonly found in information and reference products. The most advanced degree of multimedia, immersion or virtual reality, puts you in the action. The majority of modern multimedia products fall somewhere between these two extremes.*

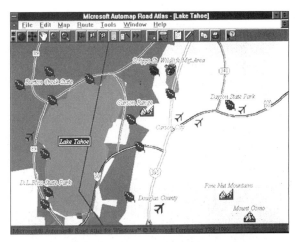

▶ *Some products, like* Microsoft Automap Road Atlas, *help you find information either in preparation for travel or just for the fun of it. Shown is Lake Tahoe, one of the places you can visit using this multimedia reference product.*

not. As a result, the interactivity of a title may not be at the level suggested or even required by the content. Therefore, while you might expect every multimedia movie to provide full virtual-reality-style immersion, many offer only basic navigation tools. On the flip side, production resources may outweigh the content. In this case, you may find the level of interactivity far exceeds the quality of the multimedia content.

There are no hard and fast rules for determining the degree of a multimedia production, although reading this book is a good first step in preparing yourself to be an educated consumer of multimedia products. The remainder of Part 1 describes the basic types of content you're likely to encounter and the corresponding degree of interactivity when you're shopping for multimedia titles. Keep in mind that each individual title is its own entity and may deviate substantially from the following guide. However, understanding the various types of multimedia content and the corresponding degree of interactivity for each will help you distinguish between hype and reality.

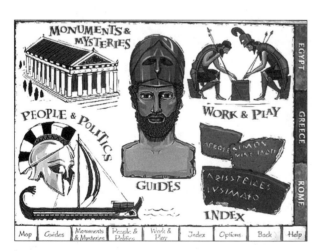

▶ *Find out about the lands our ancestors once roamed with* Microsoft Ancient Lands, *a multimedia reference product designed to give you insight into our world.*

Informational/ Reference Navigation (Lowest Degree)

Many of the today's most popular multimedia products are designed to offer fast and easy access to information. Encyclopedias, medical references, fix-it-yourself manuals, telephone books, maps, and fact books are

among the many different types of informational products available in multimedia form. The raw information in these products can include not only text and photographs, but sound and video as well. The most powerful aspect of multimedia is its ability to make even the most difficult subjects easy to understand. Using a rich mixture of media coupled with the right navigation tools, multimedia can make textual information that was once difficult — if not impossible to understand by reading a book — a joy to learn.

The ability to quickly search for a specific piece of information is the most important aspect of interactivity for informational/reference products. If the product is designed properly, users can easily search through a tremendous amount of data to find exactly what they are looking for. These search features can greatly reduce the amount of time it would normally take to find the information, while often yielding better results. In the case of a multimedia encyclopedia, for instance, you aren't required to flip through a number of pages and scan a list of names to find what you are interested in. Instead, you simply type in the *keyword* and are immediately shown the corresponding entry.

Illustrations may exist that you can bring to life. Interested in humpback whales? Don't simply read about them. Watch them dive into the great abyss, surface, and shoot water and air through their blow holes. Hear them call to one another in their wonderful whale voices. All of this is possible with good navigation tools and multimedia. But isn't there more?

keyword A word used to search for information when navigating a reference or informational product. For instance, when searching for information about humpback whales, the keywords **humpback** or **whale** could be used.

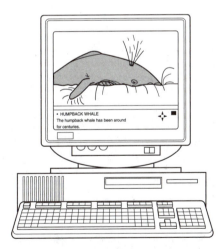

▶ *Multimedia reference products provide easy and fast access to an incredible amount of information.*

hypertext A system that links words and phrases together so you can navigate textual information in a free-form fashion that is faster and more accurate than other methods of searching for information.

Hypertext (Standard Degree)

Basic navigation tools just scratch the surface of multimedia ore. Dig deeper in many informational/reference products and you may find the fantastically powerful feature known as *hypertext*. Though it may sound like something gleaned from a bad *Star Trek* episode, hypertext is a modern information tool that is not limited to multimedia products. Hypertext systems link words and phrases together in a way that makes it possible to navigate textual information in a free-form fashion, which is faster and more accurate than standard text-search tools, while providing capabilities not otherwise possible.

▶ With Microsoft Dinosaurs *reference product, you can get immediate answers to your questions about these fantastic creatures that ruled the earth millions of years ago.*

Since words, phrases, and even entire pages of text are linked together to aid navigation, hypertext systems make it possible to search for a word or combination of words in free-form fashion, increasing the likelihood of your finding what you are looking for. For example, while looking for *humpback whale* in a reference product containing a few hundred thousand pages of electronic text, you might find that a standard search technique results in several hundred matches.

With hypertext, instead of simply looking for the words "humpback whale," you would also indicate what type of information you are looking for. When you search for humpback whale and feeding habits and plankton all at once, a hypertext system returns all the information about humpback whales feeding on plankton rather than all nonrelated occurrences of the words "humpback whale."

Hypertext provides enhanced searching capabilities through links, but it goes even further. Items that maintain links may be navigated in a manner that has become the hallmark of hypertext systems. Each item that contains a link, or a "hot" item, is differentiated from the standard text by color, or style, or both.

Imagine the text you are now reading is actually in hypertext form. Individual words or phrases that contain links to other words or phrases are bright red and bold. You immediately recognize the items having links, although you are able to continue reading the text as normal. But since you are interested in knowing more about one of the red, bold words, you use your computer mouse to position the cursor (also called pointer) over the word, and, by pressing the mouse button, click on it. You are immediately taken to a different page in the book where you can read the link. You can return to your starting point by clicking on the link again, or by clicking on any red words that interest you.

Suppose you are still looking for information on **humpback whales**. Begin by clicking on that phrase, and you are instantly shown the basic description of these wonderful mammals. While reading the description, you click on

▶ *Brøderbund's* Maps'n'Facts *reference product helps you find places on the map and interesting facts related to each location.*

▶ Microsoft Dogs *delivers instant information on every known breed of dog.*

▶ *Mantis Development Corporation's World Wide Web browser enhancement allows you to navigate the Web portion of the Internet by sight alone. This system uses professionally designed graphics to provide point-and-click hypermedia navigation of the best Web sites around the globe.*

the red word **feeding** and are given a page or two of information on the feeding habits of humpback whales, including their love of plankton. Click on the red word **plankton,** and you leap to the definition of that word and are no longer viewing information about humpback whales.

You could return to your previous location if you wanted. But you don't, and instead decide to play intellectual hopscotch with your new-found friend: hypertext. Hop around at will, finding out as much about a particular subject as you'd like and then branch out and hop in an entirely different direction. Once you have begun to navigate a hypertext system, you'll likely have a tough time stopping. Learning with hypertext is effortless, powerful, and addictive.

Hypermedia (Advanced Degree)

When a product contains more than text, as all multimedia products do, it is possible to provide a hypermedia system using the same principles found with hypertext. Photographs, video, sound, and text can be linked to one another to form a system of interconnected media. These linked media types can be navigated in the same fashion as hypertext.

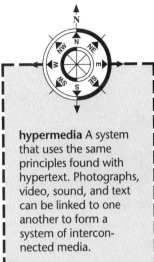

hypermedia A system that uses the same principles found with hypertext. Photographs, video, sound, and text can be linked to one another to form a system of interconnected media.

Using our familiar humpback whale example, let's extend the hypertext concept to include all media. You might begin by performing a search on the words humpback whale. In addition to text matches being reported in a list, all media types containing a link or reference to humpback whales are also shown. You can watch video, listen to audio, and view photographs if available. But what makes *hypermedia* truly powerful is its ability to allow free-form navigation.

For example, suppose you find the picture of the humpback's massive tail, or fluke, intriguing. You might also find this particular photograph linked to an entire series of photographs detailing the differences in whale flukes among the species. One of these photographs might be linked to a movie that shows a whale slapping its mighty fluke on the surface of the water with great force and noise which, of course, you hear. And while watching the movie you see that it is linked to an audio track of Jacques Cousteau explaining why these giant mammals slap the water so, and you listen to the audio track. Then you notice that the audio track is linked to an entire section of information dedicated to Cousteau and his underwater adventures, and so you're off in another direction, simply following your interests.

With hypermedia, just as with hypertext, you are able to navigate information in a free-form manner that fits your style and needs. Hypermedia, however, delivers a wealth of visual and audible material that cannot be achieved by text alone.

Almost There: Interactive Movies

In order to adequately describe the highest degree of multimedia, it is helpful to begin first with an example of a typical multimedia product that comes very close: the *interactive movie*. While initially you may not think this degree of multimedia could be much different from using a VCR or laserdisc player to navigate a movie, closer inspection reveals the truth about interactive movies.

A standard movie is presented to the viewer as a sequence of related information, in which audio and video are intermingled to convey the director's message or vision. We usually watch movies in a linear fashion, from beginning to end, with an occasional intermission or commercial break.

▶ *Learn more about the world's most dangerous creatures the safe and easy way — from the comfort of your computer. (from Microsoft's* Dangerous Creatures)

Using a VCR or laserdisc device you are able to navigate the movie with a bit more control. You can skip over parts you do not like, or rewind and replay specific scenes at will. You are also able to freeze a single frame of the movie into place using the pause feature. Yet, however convenient these capabilities may be, the movie itself remains a single, linear recording of sound and video intended to be viewed in a predetermined sequence. Because the individual frames and scenes of a movie rely on the previous frames and scenes to make sense, great confusion would result if we were to jump around the contents at random.

Suppose the various scenes of a movie were randomly scrambled, then reassembled without care. As a linear format, the movie's message or vision would also be scrambled and therefore become incomprehensible to the viewer. The predetermined sequence of scenes would be missing, making the movie utterly incoherent.

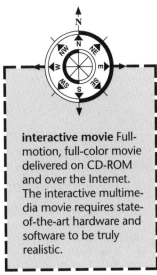

interactive movie Full-motion, full-color movie delivered on CD-ROM and over the Internet. The interactive multimedia movie requires state-of-the-art hardware and software to be truly realistic.

Contrast the standard movie with any multimedia production. In multimedia, individual blocks of information are exactly that: single, discrete "chunks" of data that may be accessed in any order without following a predetermined sequence. Each piece of information may be viewed alone, independent of the others.

And while it is possible to view any scene in any order, randomly jumping from scene to scene in a multimedia movie might be just as confusing as scrambling scenes in a traditional movie. The fundamental difference, however, lies in your ability to navigate the contents of a multimedia movie. Individual scenes are linked to related scenes, allowing you to easily explore related content. If, for instance, you are viewing a scene from the middle of a multimedia movie, you would also have the option of viewing the previous and following scenes, or any other scenes that relate in some way to the one you are currently viewing.

You might also have the ability to read or listen to a description of the current scene, accessing related information in a way not possible in a

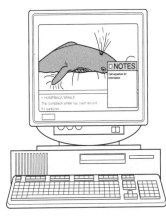

▶ *While navigating multimedia reference products, it is often possible to take notes on your experience or place bookmarks along the way that you (or others) can refer to later.*

virtual reality The ability to move about and control a multimedia experience from your own perspective and as a full participant rather than a passive viewer. Multimedia of this degree, known as immersion or virtual reality (VR), is the most advanced multimedia available and requires more than just a hefty computer system. Specialized hardware, such as video goggles and data gloves, may be required to get the full effect of some VR products.

traditional movie. While viewing a scene, you might enter personal notes by voice or keyboard for future reference or for others to read when they are at the same point in the movie. You might even place bookmarks throughout the production, allowing instant access to your favorite scenes in the future. The fundamental difference between a multimedia movie and a standard movie is your ability to navigate the contents in a free-form context without becoming completely lost or confused along the way.

Immersion/Virtual Reality (Highest Degree)

Take this concept one step further and allow the viewer to become part of the action. In this case, you don't just explore various parts of a movie, you become the central character. You aren't simply retrieving information. You're in there, fluke to fluke, with the whales. There is no linear format to follow. You are free to roam about just as you do in real life.

Confronted with the choice to walk around the lake or wade into the water? Take your pick. Threatened by a treacherous beast? Turn tail and run, or fight if you're up to it. How about trying to calm the monster with a bit of food from the backpack you filled with goodies earlier in your adventure? The choice is yours. Unlike a traditional movie, there are no preset plots or scenes. Sure, there is a limitation to what you can do. You may find that the water is so cold it turns your blood to ice, or that the beast has no interest in angel food cake. But hey, at least you can try.

Since the production is composed of many individual scenes each linked to one another, you can move about and enjoy the experience as a participant rather than a passive viewer. Multimedia of this degree, known as *immersion* or *virtual reality*, requires more than just a hefty computer system. The product must be designed for such use, with special care given to your ability to navigate the contents from your own perspective rather than that of the director. In addition, specialized hardware such as *video goggles* and *data gloves* may be required.

Video goggles provide an astounding element of realism: Items are viewed in 3-D and move into and out of view in response to head movements. Data gloves make it possible for users to use their hands as they would in real life: Items can be picked up and examined, thrown or caught, broken or repaired.

The design of a virtual reality product also dictates your ability to interact with the world you enter. If the water was too cold, it was because the designers of the product intended it to be. It could have been made boiling hot or even covered with ice, or both. There are no boundaries in virtual reality, just those imposed by the designers of the product and the limitations of the technology.

Immersed in a new and strange world you might find that you look like a bird, and by flapping your wings you can fly! Up, up and away you soar, looking down at the small triangular red planet below. Past your head zip other birds, some big and some small, each grinning broadly and singing opera in Latin with full tenor voices while fashioning baby clothes with chopsticks and yarn. Hey, this is virtual reality. Anything can happen.

data glove A highly specialized piece of computer equipment that looks like a normal glove, yet when worn transmits hand movements into the computer.

video goggles A highly specialized piece of computer equipment that looks similar to ski goggles (or in some cases, a streamlined motorcycle helmet), yet transmits head movements into the computer and video images to the eyes of the user.

Where Do We See Multimedia?

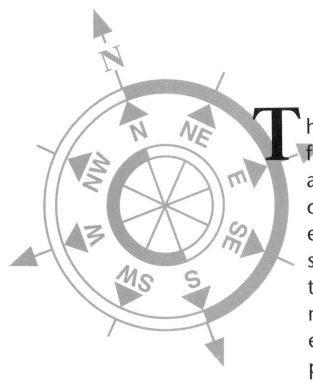

The most obvious places you'll find multimedia are in the areas we've already discussed: computer systems, home entertainment systems, television, and the movies. But with the advent of CD-ROM technology and the continuing exponential growth in computing power, personal computers and home entertainment systems are clearly in the vanguard of interactive multimedia technology.

Television and the Big Screen

Just because you can't interact with the media presented on TV or the big screen doesn't mean you can't use it to view multimedia presentations. On a daily basis you are exposed to a wide range of multimedia presentations, unless you don't have a television or always have it turned off. Where is all this multimedia on TV? Commercials, of course. Most of the snazzy, whiz-bang images

multimedia presentation A multimedia work you watch but do not participate in.

interactivity The ability to navigate the contents of a multimedia product, giving you some degree of control over it. With an interactive product, you are in control, telling the product where you want to be, what you want to see, and how you want to experience it. If it's not interactive, it's not true multimedia by today's standards.

you see and nifty sound effects you hear are courtesy of multimedia technology. You can't navigate these multimedia presentations, but isn't it nice enough just to watch them? Advertisers think so, and spend millions of dollars on state-of-the-art multimedia commercials to show you what great products they have.

Did you ever think you'd see credit cards dance and a gas pump tango with a Mercedes? How about a lively bottle of breath freshener swinging from vine to vine in the jungle, hunting for bad breath germs to destroy? These are a few of the more memorable television commercials that use multimedia to grab our attention, but there are many others that are a joy to watch because they are so visually compelling. One of my favorites is the razor blade commercial that shows a man shaving while his face is continually transformed into the faces of many other men, illustrating that this one razor blade can handle many types of faces. You soon see that even the most difficult-to-shave face is no problem for this razor, as the man's head is transformed into a rectangular block with eyes, ears, and nose. Too far out there? Perhaps you prefer the commercial in which polar bears drink soda while ice skating arm in arm, often seen around the Christmas season as one beverage company uses multimedia to advertise the universal appeal of its soft drink. Whatever your taste, there's a multimedia flavor to match.

Be aware, however, that a dazzling multimedia commercial doesn't automatically guarantee that the advertised product is also fantastic. Advertisers use the power of multimedia to sell you their products. Perfectly ordinary products are often advertised using stunning multimedia commercials, so it's a good idea to keep your guard up when it comes to this new method of communicating with consumers. You should keep two things in mind as multimedia continues to make its way into the public arena: 1) multimedia presentations are extremely expensive to create and 2) product advertisers have the deepest pockets and the most compelling reasons to use multimedia, namely profit. Knowing this, sit back and enjoy these amazing and entertaining commercials for their sheer beauty and creativity, yet keep it all in perspective: they are product advertisements.

multimedia A computer product composed of two or more media (sound, video, photography, animation, text, and so on) with which the user can interact.

It would be truly disheartening if commercials were the only place we saw multimedia, and so it's nice to know you can go to the movies for a gigantic dose of the stuff. Watch Arnold Schwarzenegger blow up everything in his path in the action-packed movie *True Lies,* while comforted by the fact that no real countries were demolished in the process. And you can rest easy knowing Arnold isn't actually the ultra-violent cyborg he portrays in the futuristic *Terminator* movies; it's multimedia that makes his half-man, half-machine character so life-like and realistic.

If massive carnage and destruction aren't your style, sit back and marvel as Tom Hanks chats with JFK in the Academy Award winning blockbuster *Forrest Gump* or witness Jim Carey's head explode in color and shape after donning a primitive tribal mask in the visually dazzling film *The Mask.* And don't think for a moment that old-fashioned movie techniques such as stop-motion photography and heavy makeup are at the center of all those actors who've been transformed into vampires and werewolves in modern day horror flicks; it's magic — multimedia magic.

As a general rule of thumb, you can just about guarantee that if something you're watching at home or at the movies looks unbelievable, it's thanks to multimedia. And while these productions don't allow you to control the action, they certainly give you something exciting to watch. And isn't that all we really want, anyway?

Information Kiosks

Get a grip — the best multimedia isn't something you watch, it's something you do! While every multimedia product has the capacity to simply present information, even if it's as simple as a self-playing video game demonstration in which you do nothing but watch, the real power of multimedia is in interactivity. Even those products that make multimedia presentations possible offer interactivity; somebody must first interact with the product in order to create a presentation in the first place. In this case, however, the end result is a presentation that the general public watches but does not participate in.

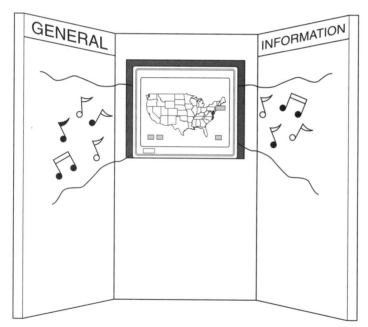

▶ *Located in public areas, information kiosks provide a relatively low degree of interactivity using a touch-sensitive computer screen housed in a large plastic body. People navigate the contents of these special-purpose multimedia devices by simply touching the images and text that appear on screen.*

Have you ever stopped at an information kiosk in a shopping mall or airport? How about at the car dealership? Video store? Real estate agent? Music store? Well, maybe you haven't used them, but you've seen them: those just-below-eye-level things that look like a bizarre cross between an oil drum and a television set. They may occasionally seem to shout out random statements to grab your attention as you pass by and, once they have it, attempt to get to know you by asking a few questions such as "What is your name?" and "Where do you live?" You know what I'm talking about. Admit it, we've all been there.

Information kiosks are really just informational multimedia products packaged inside industrial-strength plastic containers built to take the rigors of public beatings. Kiosks feature touch-sensitive video displays to present and allow interaction with their contents. Navigation is achieved by simply pressing the images and text displayed on the screen. Did you just get off the plane and want to know where to find good food in an unfamiliar city? Forget asking someone. Just saunter on over to the nearest kiosk and see which restaurants paid big bucks to have their menus made available to the fingertips of millions. After a quick and intimate session of "20 Questions," a list of fine eateries within walking distance of your hotel is printed on the spot. You may even be able to make reservations right from the kiosk if you're lucky. My favorite information kiosks, however, take the place of hotel concierges. These *kiosk concierges* tell you all you'd like to know about the area you're visiting and often include food and entertainment information as well.

The best part about a kiosk concierge is that once you've got its attention, it's all yours. No people cutting in line, or if you're on the telephone, no one breaking through on call waiting. You have its undivided attention and won't feel uncomfortable asking what might seem to be simple questions. Ask away, without bothering to desperately scribble down instructions by hand. Simply take your printed instructions when ready and thank the hard-working and considerate kiosk. Then you can swagger on out to the cab and hand the driver a fresh printout, which gives crystal-clear instructions on how to get to wherever you're going.

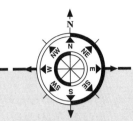

information kiosks
Informational multimedia products packaged inside industrial-strength plastic containers approximately 5 feet high by 3 feet wide, built to take the rigors of public use. Information kiosks, or simply kiosks, feature touch-sensitive video displays to present and allow interaction with their contents. Navigation is achieved by pressing the images and text displayed on the screen.

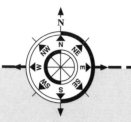

kiosk concierge
Information kiosks typically located in hotel lobbies and dedicated to providing information normally available through the hotel concierge. These kiosks typically supply information about local restaurants, entertainment, and transportation.

While television and movies offer compelling multimedia presentations, kiosks go the extra mile and let you interact with their contents. Here, you navigate a multimedia product for specific information. Kiosks usually sport both hypertext and hypermedia technology in one easy-to-use package. Don't expect to be blown away by dazzling multimedia presentations when using a kiosk, however. For the most part these systems are purely informational, having only text, low resolution graphics, and occasional audio snippets. But brace yourself for the snazzy multimedia commercials, which will undoubtedly start to show up on these systems. Kiosk manufacturers know the value of an advertisement vehicle placed smack-dab in the public eye. As soon as the technology is cheap enough, the ads will start rolling in. It's only a matter of time before New York City's Times Square-style electronic billboard advertisements begin to appear on public kiosks across the country.

▶ Once you have found something of interest using an information kiosk, many will print it out for you on the spot! This feature is especially convenient when it comes to directions, where the alternative is frantically scribbling down the information using a pen and paper.

Commuter TV

I live and work in Boston, a hotbed of multimedia technology. Kiosks abound, as do commuters who ride the subway into the city for work every morning. Over the past few years, *Commuter TV* was introduced. Now, in addition to the fellow playing a harmonica at Kenmore Square and the duo strumming acoustic guitars to accompany their moving rendition of "Down By the Boardwalk," subway riders can peer up at television monitors for a glimpse of our country's future. Nothing spectacular is to be seen on Commuter TV — at least not yet. Moving video isn't even available, just still images of information such as the current time and temperature with a variety of special effect dissolves and wipes when shifting between them.

However, these devices give us something interesting to watch while waiting for the train. And although they could offer more public interest items (such as photographs of local runaways and missing children) to balance out the advertisements that regularly appear, Commuter TV is a great example of a public kiosk that provides useful information. Now I no longer need to ask a stranger for the time to confirm that I'm running behind schedule; I simply glance up at Commuter TV for the current time, at which point I also see the weather report forecasts heavy rain and realize my umbrella is at home, probably alongside my watch.

Consumer Beware

Keep you're guard up as the razzle-dazzle hits the screens and streets. Just because a product comes wrapped in a slick package doesn't automatically make it a better buy, nor does it mean you should rush out and get it. Today, where image influences reality, the ability to create an incredible image is possible with multimedia technology. Remember, good looking doesn't always equal better.

Commuter TV
Specially equipped television sets found in many subway stations across the nation that display general information such as the current time and temperature, in addition to advertisements. Commuter TV devices are used only to display information and do not allow viewers to interact with the broadcast.

▶ *Subways across the country are being equipped with Commuter TV, a multimedia presentation device that displays general information such as time, temperature, and the weather. The subway rider has something interesting to look at while waiting for the train and also gets useful information.*

▶ *Don't be fooled! Consumers are often wrongly convinced that slick and fancy packaging means a better quality product, when generic brands are usually just as good if not better. The same is true for many multimedia products, where expensive and exciting packaging often is the only worthwhile part of a product.*

Consider for a moment the food industry. Products are often sold under both a generic label and a fancy, name-brand label — and the only difference is the packaging. The same is true in the drug industry, where generic medicines cost a fraction of the name-brand products, although they may contain exactly the same active ingredients. Yet consumers often buy products that come in fancy packages simply because of their visual appeal, despite the fact that the generic brands are usually just as good. Realizing up-front that a product's image doesn't always reflect its worth will help make you a more discerning consumer as multimedia advertisements explode on the scene.

Most of the multimedia technology we see on a daily basis is primarily oriented toward entertainment and advertisement, although kiosks do offer information at your fingertips. Yet, beyond this basic technology lies a world of multimedia products that actually do something for you.

Interactive Shopping

Today's Home Shopping Network has pioneered the ability to shop from the comfort of your living room, and is another good example of multimedia presentation used on the television. Now, take this concept a bit further. Jazz it up as only multimedia can do and place it in the form of an interactive kiosk. Here you have an advertising machine that can be placed in almost any public area, where nearly anything can be purchased at the touch of a button after inserting a credit card. It brings an entirely new twist to impulse shopping, doesn't it?

But millions of consumers would never consider ordering something like an engagement ring or fine food from the same place that sells the "Salad Shooter" and "Garden Weasel." In a few years these clearinghouse style operations will soon find themselves competing head-to-head with traditional manufacturers as televised and kiosk-based interactive multimedia begins to provide direct contact with consumers without the overhead of store space and sales

▶ *America Online offers shop-at-home convenience through their on-line services.*

staff. When Tiffany and Cartier not only advertise engagement rings using this technology, but also offer the ability to browse through the various styles of gems available *and* allow the suitor to tinker with a few "what-if" payment plans while applying for credit on the spot, even the eternally cautious will buy. Who knows? Proposals delivered on one knee might soon be replaced by proposals delivered by overnight courier. And as surely as the number of impulse proposals grows, so too will the number of interactive divorce courts.

Effective interactive shopping through your television or through a kiosk is at least five years away, however, and so we'll have to make do with variations on the theme until then. Take for example the "Create-A-Greeting" machines now popping up across the nation. Entirely devoted to greeting cards, these systems let you design a custom card for any occasion. Looking like a glorified information kiosk, these machines take the concept one step further by delivering a tangible product. You navigate the contents just as you would any kiosk: the difference is the content itself.

After you have selected a card style, appropriate text, and a few predesigned graphics, you then type in the name of the recipient. You can even enter your own name together with a personalized

▶ *Commerical on-line services such as Prodigy already allow you to purchase a wide array of products from the comfort of your home computer.*

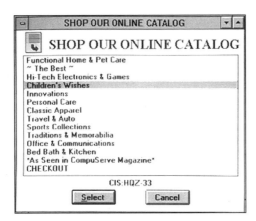

▶ *Browsing the aisles of a store in an "electronic mall" is easy! Here we have entered a store on CompuServe, where we can get information on products and place an order directly from the computer.*

salutation for an added dash of panache. When you're happy with your creation, the final product is printed on thick, heavy paper. Bingo. You've just created your own greeting card.

Create-A-Greeting machines are an ingenious twist to traditional kiosks, but interactive machines like these are relatively few and far between these days, and the products they generate are often more expensive than the pre-multimedia form of the product. Nevertheless, these machines usher in a new wave of consumer goods: on-the-spot customization and delivery of products without having to wait in line or seek assistance from a salesperson.

Although it won't be long before you'll be able to walk up to a kiosk and order nearly any product you can think of using only your index finger and a credit card, the promise of instant delivery for most items is impractical at best. Your order will likely be delivered the next business day by a courier such as Federal Express, provided the item is in stock or can be created in time. But that in itself is a major advance over how we shop for goods today, just as the modern information kiosk is a major advancement over pulling into the nearest roadside gas station for directions or dining advice.

Remember, this technology is in its infancy and is at roughly the same stage in its development as the first Model-T cars rolling off the Ford assembly line so many years ago. Information technology, however, matures and advances at an incredibly faster rate than industrial technology. Ford didn't go from the Model-T to the Mustang overnight; it took over 50 years for the technology to ripen. Rest assured, however, it won't be much more than a handful of years before you can order dinner from your favorite restaurant using a remote control pointed at your television, or order clothing, movies, and vacations in the same way.

In the short term, devices similar to the Create-A-Greeting machines provide convenient access to easily printed and instantly deliverable items such as movie and concert tickets. It may not be earth shattering, but it works and sure beats waiting in line.

Multimedia in the Office

Overwhelmingly, corporate multimedia comes in the form of presentation rather than interaction. However, the difference between previously mentioned multimedia presentations (specifically, television and movies) and those found in the corporate world boils down to control: Here, you create the presentation yourself by interacting with multimedia software designed for such use. The interactive aspect of presentation software isn't intended to provide an exciting multimedia experience; it is provided only to give you the ability to create a multimedia presentation that others can then sit back and watch. The focus here is on creating multimedia presentations for others to view, not on interacting with a product for the sheer joy of it.

The ultimate tool for creating jazzy handouts, slides, and multimedia presentations, the personal computer has changed the face of corporate communications. Nearly gone are the days of overhead projectors and photocopied materials. Today, most of corporate

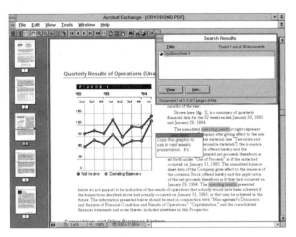

America wouldn't consider distributing such primitive materials for presentation purposes. Full-color printouts, slides, and stunning multimedia presentations are now commonplace, and stereo-quality sound pumping from Bose speakers while 3-D bar charts dance to the beat are almost expected when the company president delivers a presentation.

▶ Adobe Acrobat *has become a popular product for distributing corporate information. Many companies use* Adobe Acrobat *to create hypertext and hypermedia multimedia products that contain a wealth of textual and graphical information.*

Trade shows and conferences run amok in multimedia technology, again primarily presentation. For the most part, business people only need to see the images and hear the sounds rather than be part of the presentation. Noninteractive presentations are the time-honored foundation of corporate communications, as radio and television commercials have long proven. Who would have thought that soap operas would be created for the sole purpose of stealing the attention of housewives long enough to sell them laundry detergents and cleaning goods? They don't call them *soap* operas for nothing. When it comes to selling goods, presentations are extremely effective. And they are even more effective given the flash and pizzazz of multimedia.

Video Conferencing

While today the majority of corporate multimedia is used for some form of presentation, either internally or for public consumption, slowly but surely the workplace is beginning to utilize interactive multimedia. For instance, more and more companies are exploring the benefits of *video conferencing*. With video conferencing you can, without leaving the comfort of your desk or company meeting room, participate in a conference with people across the street or across the world. Your image and voice are broadcast to all members participating in the conference, while you in turn can see and hear everyone else. Video conferencing is like a two-way television show in which you are a participant. Imagine your television attached to a speaker-phone and you've just about got video-conferencing. Toss in a video camera that is focused tightly on your face while it broadcasts every rolled eye and smirk to others in the conference, and you've got it. You can see and hear everyone, and they can see and hear you.

video conferencing
Conducting conferences with people at various locations. Your image and voice are broadcast to all members participating in the conference, while you in turn can see and hear everyone else.

If this sounds like a lot of expensive equipment just to hold a meeting, imagine for a moment if everyone had to pack their bags and fly across the country, or the world, instead. The savings gained by avoiding just a few business trips pays for the equipment. And since only certain conference rooms need the equipment, overall savings can be great. An added plus is the time saved. Rather than dedicating your entire day or week to attend a meeting out of state or country, you can simply step into the video-conferencing room at the set meeting time and return to your daily grind when it's over. No travel, hotel, jet lag

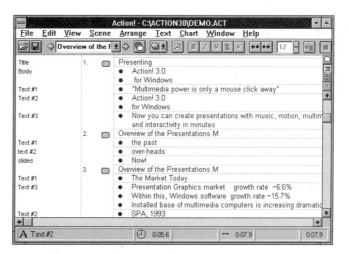

▶ To help organize presentations and keep them on track, many multimedia presentation software products include outline capabilities. Although a presentation is taking place, the person delivering it can view both the multimedia presentation and the outline to ensure all topics are being discussed in appropriate detail.

or headache. Thanks to these advantages, video conferencing is beginning to bloom in corporate environments, further shortening the distance between companies and customers while improving the overall bottom line. But where is the interactivity?

Many video conference systems include electronic white boards that broadcast to all participants whatever is written on them. With electronic white boards, all the elements of a real meeting are in place. The only hurdle, however, is the ability to distribute hand-outs. Of course these materials can be sent via courier to all members of the meeting. But the problem with this approach is not only the high expense incurred using couriers, but also the danger of last-minute changes or additions to the materials that arrive too late for delivery. And in the business world, last-minute changes and additions are as common as the handshake and familiar "don't worry, everything's under control" clasp on the back.

▶ *Many multimedia presentation products use a timeline to schedule events that occur during a particular presentation. Graphics, moving video, sound effects, music, and text all are arranged in relation to the timeline, ensuring that each item is presented in the proper order and at the exact time needed during the presentation.*

Groupware

Enter *groupware*, specialized computer software that allows people to share electronic documents, images, voice, and even video. With groupware, everyone receives the changes and additions as they happen. In fact, one of the biggest advantages with groupware lies in its ability to allow a number of people to view and edit a single document at once. Imagine using groupware to produce your company's annual report. Each section of the report requires the combined input from a variety of people in every division of the company: finance, marketing, sales, distribution, customer service, and so on. With groupware, each party contributes their own piece of the pie using the computer at their desks. Since everyone involved can see and make changes to the main document using their own computer, the power of collaboration allows the various contributors to refine and add to the document as a unified group without leaving their desks. Some groupware products even include computerized video-conferencing, further breaking down the barriers of time and space.

groupware Specialized software that allows people on different computers to share electronic documents, images, voice, and even video.

These are just a few of the glitzy uses of multimedia in the office environment, although a multitude of other products are being used on a daily basis. Without a doubt, multimedia technology has begun to shape the way we do business. It may not be as splashy or exciting as the entertainment world, but it is just as important and has far-reaching implications in how we communicate and interact with one another in a corporate environment. And while it may seem that this new technology will ultimately isolate people from one another, many groupware products provide the electronic equivalent of our real-word office coffee pot and water cooler. These "virtual gatherings" provide an electronic area where people can come together to chat, share work and personal issues, and even arrange for off-site gatherings

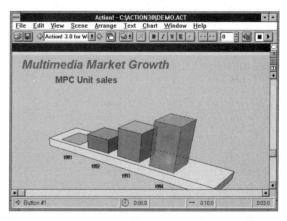

▶ *The ability to create stunning multimedia presentations is easy when you use a product built for such purposes, such as Macromedia's Action!. Multimedia presentation software products, popular in the corporate world, can jazz up any presentation and bring otherwise dry subjects to life.*

and office parties. Such capabilities are provided for a number of reasons, the most important of which is that as we begin to shift from an industrial society to an information society, one constant remains: people need people.

Multimedia at School

The most staggering implications of multimedia technology are to be found in education. With hypertext and hypermedia systems, students have instant access to a world of information without the need for traditional libraries or the personal attention of an instructor. For almost every subject taught in school, a multitude of corresponding interactive products containing text, photographs, video, speech, and music exist. Free to consume information at whatever rate desired, students will undoubtedly feel the impact of multimedia more profoundly than those outside the classroom. As generations of students chomp at the silver spoon of multimedia, we will witness a revolution in the way humans learn and think.

Youth's natural hunger for knowledge, coupled with a massive stimulation of the mind brought about by exposure to instantaneously retrieved information in multimedia form, will, over the coming generations, ultimately change the way human beings use their minds. This is inevitable. Just as mankind's quest for knowledge throughout his tenure on earth has expanded his ability to think and reason, so too will a few hundred years of multimedia learning.

▶ *Challenge your knowledge of math by counting, adding, subtracting, dividing, multiplying, and more with MECC's edutainment product* Troggle Trouble Math. *No flash cards. No drills.*

Multimedia, however, promises to deliver far greater intellectual growth in a much shorter period of time than we have ever experienced. And today, many of our nation's students have taken the first steps of this profound journey.

▶ *Edutainment products like Brøderbund's* Where in the World is Carmen Sandiego? *make learning a breeze.*

While the ultimate impact of this technology on the human race won't be known for generations to come, it is important to realize that today our children are firing the first shots of this revolution in classrooms across the nation. This isn't happening in every school system, of course, but in many. This revolution in education will continue to advance as success is reported from the front lines. But, just as in any revolution, there are many obstacles to overcome before we can pat ourselves on the back and take in the sweet smell of victory.

Educational equipment standards must be agreed upon, multimedia learning tools must be assessed for viability, and the use of computers and multimedia must become part of the core curriculum for all school systems. All of this — in addition to the funding of necessary equipment — must be tackled by our school systems and government before the promise of universal learning with multimedia can become a reality in every classroom. And since learning with multimedia is such a radical departure from the chalkboard and textbook approach, teachers themselves must learn how to teach a new generation of students using these new systems. Resistance will be found at every turn, every corridor, every classroom. Nobody said it was going to be easy. But what good is a revolution without spirited resistance?

▶ *Use your powers of deduction in Brøderbund's* Where in the World is Carmen Sandiego?, *and learn geography in the process.*

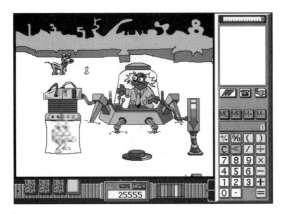

▶ *Use your math skills to help find Dr. Frankentroggle and rescue the missing Muncher in MECC's edutainment program,* Toggle Trouble Math.

Still, there are a number of small battles being won everyday in classrooms across the country. Some schools have stretched their grant dollars to cover the cost of multimedia equipment and titles, some have made alliances with local libraries and businesses to gain access to the equipment and expertise they cannot afford. Many colleges have added introductory computer courses to their required curriculum, while a great number of parents contribute to the cause personally by augmenting their child's education using multimedia in the home. Without a common set of standards, however, there will remain a significant imbalance among students across the nation with regard to the quality of education they are receiving with multimedia. However, if only one thing can be said with certainty at this point, it is that students truly love learning when the proper mixture of education and entertainment is applied.

Multimedia at Home

Chances are this is the place that appeals to you most when it comes to using multimedia. Sure, you may use presentation forms of multimedia at the office or, in the case of parents, your children may already be using multimedia at school. But for most of us, home is where the heart is. This is where you'll use the latest and greatest multimedia products, each at your own pace, and with the comfort of sinking deep into the experience without worrying about deadlines and meetings cutting in on your time. And best of all, you get to choose which titles you use.

Home multimedia is most often experienced on a personal computer, although a great number of people also own a *home entertainment system* such Atari, Nintendo, and Sega. While these game systems are certainly fun to use and provide excellent quality video games, they don't provide the rich breadth of products found with the personal computer. Whereas game systems are focused only on games, the personal computer gives you access to every type of multimedia you can imagine.

home entertainment system Small, relatively inexpensive devices that attach to a television and provide entertainment primarily in the form of video games. Extremely popular among teenagers, Atari, Nintendo, and Sega are the most common home entertainment systems in use today.

With a multimedia personal computer, you may choose to bring your work home from time to time. In this case, multimedia in the home would be the same as you experience it in the office. Or, you may decide to augment your children's education, having the same multimedia products they use at school also available in your home. With a personal computer, you can boost your own productivity and enhance your children's education all from the comfort of home. At the same time, you have the option of enjoying the scores of

▶ *Origin's* BioForge *is a multimedia action game that takes you far beyond the experience you can have with standard home entertainment systems.*

multimedia products on the market, which may have nothing to do with work or school. With a home multimedia computer, it's your choice. Some types of multimedia are meant to educate, others to

entertain, and still others offer sheer productivity gains without teaching or entertaining at all. Whatever your preference, there is a type of multimedia to match.

Edutainment

The very best educational products are those that not only teach students, but also entertain them in the process. Available today in a variety of multimedia forms, these tools are so successful that they have established a unique category of computer products with a name all their own: *edutainment*. Learning with edutainment is a blast. You not only learn, but you have fun at the same time. So much fun, in fact, that sometimes you forget you are learning. It seems that in edutainment, educators may have found their Holy Grail.

▶ *Learning math is fun with Brøderbund's* Math Workshop *edutainment software. You'll never look at fractions the same way!*

Tapping into the power of the joy of learning, edutainment combines the exciting elements found in entertainment products while adding the value of a learning experience. For example, an edutainment product for mathematics might combine the thrill of a video game with the repetition needed when memorizing multiplication tables: When the player, or student, runs out of ammunition in a shoot-'em-up scenario, he must quickly answer a multiplication problem. The longer he takes, the less ammo he'll receive and the closer his enemy will come to taking the upper hand. Not surprisingly, most students playing a game like this have no problem memorizing the multiplication tables, while their chalkboard counterparts struggle to keep from falling asleep during class. But not all students like their math to come in blow-'em-to-smithereens style video games.

For these pupils, entertainment might be a "Who Dunnit?" style mystery, where they walk quietly around an old, dusty mansion and collect clues to help identify the perpetrator of a given crime. Of course the butler did it, but in order to prove it the student must solve a few dozen math problems wrapped in the guise of a riddle. Here the entertaining elements of suspense and mystery are combined with mathematics to bring learning to life and encourage students to spend more time exploring the joy of learning than simply memorizing numbers.

Going beyond traditional course materials, many truly innovative edutainment products are emerging for the education market. *Wagon Train 1848* is a great example, although it has been

The astronauts floated in space. They worked all day to repair the satellite. Then, they saw two spaceships coming. "Maybe they can help us!" one of the astronauts yelled.

▶ *Write and illustrate your own storybooks with MECC's edutainment program,* Storybook Weaver Deluxe. *A text-to-speech feature even let users hear their stories read aloud to them in English or Spanish.*

▶ *The inspiration for many of today's multimedia edutainment products, MECC's* Wagon Trail 1848 *has been used for years in classrooms across the country to teach children communication skills, deduction and reasoning skills, and group cooperation all while they learn about the Old West.*

around for several years (and will hopefully be around for many more). An interactive learning experience designed to be used by an entire classroom at once, *Wagon Train 1848* transports students back to the days of covered wagons and an undiscovered America. Students break up into small groups of three or four, each group sitting at a computer. Every computer system running *Wagon Train 1848* is connected to one another, or networked, allowing the students to play the game and communicate through the computer. Through the computer, each group of students quickly realizes that they are sitting in a covered wagon, part of an old-fashioned wagon train. Their classmates are in the other wagons, and together they make up the entire wagon train. Their goal is to head west and settle the unsettled. Some are motivated by the gold rush, others by the free land and open spaces, and still others simply by the challenge of exploring the untamed west. In any case, the students must work together to pull it off and make it across the land safely.

The *Wagon Train 1848* simulation doesn't begin and end in just one classroom session, but over a series of sessions. These student pioneers are given a certain amount of food, water and provisions, and more challenges than you might expect. As their wagon train slowly trundles across the great expanse of the wild west, they must work with one another when making almost every major decision. Should they go this way or that? Do the Indians up ahead look friendly? If so, should they trade muskets for stallions since their horses are getting too tired to keep up the pace? All of these decisions and the communication skills necessary to arrive at their ultimate destination teach

▶ *School children must work together if their wagon train is to survive the rigors of the Wild West.*

invaluable skills to young students. *Wagon Train 1848* provides a stimulating multimedia learning experience that most traditional students couldn't even imagine if they simply read a description of wagon trains in the old west, and in the process teaches invaluable decision-making and communication skills.

▶ *Some types of multimedia are meant to educate, others to entertain, and still others offer sheer productivity gains without teaching or entertaining at all. Whatever your preference, there is a type of multimedia to match.* (*from MECC's* Amazon Trail)

The company that created *Wagon Train 1848*, MECC (Minnesota Educational Computing Corporation), specializes in edutainment software and offers a number of other multimedia products that follow in the same vein. *Oregon Trail*, *Yukon Trail*, and *Amazon Trail* are all fine multimedia products that put you in the seat of the action, while delivering a valuable learning experience in the process.

Entertainment

Sometimes you don't want to learn at all, no matter how easy or interesting it may be. Step back, Dirty Harry, and hand me the joystick. It's time to beat the living tar out of everything in sight, guilty or innocent. It's time for *Mortal Kombat*!

Entertainment products don't even try to pretend they're teaching something useful, something you can carry with you and draw upon for strength through life's sorted twists and turns. Don't kid yourself; this is pure fun, however you slice it. Some like to run around and blow everything up in Rambo-style action games, while

entertainment
Multimedia products designed to be used for pleasure, rather than learning purposes. Arcade, mystery, and adventure games are just a few examples of entertainment products.

others prefer the strategic challenge of multimedia chess or world domination with *Risk*. Sports buffs want to box or play baseball and hockey. Tinkering types might want to design an ecosystem and watch it thrive or perish as it matures. And some simply want to explore virtual worlds, to see what is to be seen without concern for time or space.

Take your pick; the entertainment industry has a flavor to suit every taste. And while most people might associate home entertainment only with game systems such as Atari, Nintendo, and Sega, the multimedia computer is a mighty force to be reckoned with in the entertainment word. With high resolution graphics, enormous computing power, and the proliferation of multimedia entertainment titles for personal computers, home entertainment no longer requires your television and a joystick or paddle.

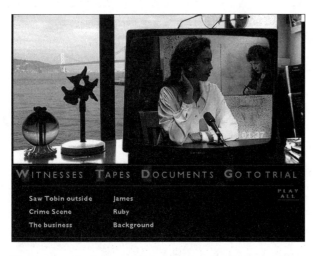

▶ *Players find themselves surrounded by suspicion and intrigue as the lead role in Brøderbund's* In The First Degree, *an interactive game for adults due to hit the shelves in September 1995.*

Whether for game systems or multimedia computers, today's entertainment products often feature the highest degree of multimedia available to the general public. A tremendous market exists for multimedia entertainment, and demand dictates supply. Hundreds upon millions of dollars are pumped into the development of state-of-the-art entertainment products, particularly those created for distribution on CD-ROM.

With CD-ROM, a unprecedented amount of multimedia can be stored on a single disc.

Simply pop the CD-ROM into your home entertainment system or computer and away you go. Animated actors, stunning graphics, stereo quality sound, and even full motion video all come together to blow your virtual socks off. Multimedia prior to CD-ROM was simply impractical. It would take over 600 traditional computer floppy disks to equal the storage capacity of a single CD-ROM. Can you imagine shuffling these disks in and out of your computer as a game is played, each of which is needed at various stages of play? And you thought tennis elbow was painful.

Thanks to CD-ROM, an entire entertainment industry has exploded onto the scene practically out of thin air. In fact, second only to television, home entertainment is the area in which you're most likely to see multimedia in action. It's a booming industry, with new titles being introduced in droves every day. Some games even

▶ *Fore! Take a swing at multimedia golf with Electronic Arts'* PGA Tour Golf Playstation.

▶ *Perhaps the most visually stunning and creative game to date,* Myst *breaks new ground as an entertainment product. As beautiful as it is original, the purpose of* Myst *is to simply explore a new and wonderful world.*

span several CD-ROMs, providing the storage space needed for an entire full motion movie with all the advantages of interactivity. By far, entertainment is the most exciting place you'll find multimedia. But before you rush out and invest in an armful of products, there's one more place you should know about.

the Internet A vast, globally connected computer network developed by the United States government after World War II. Although originally designed to provide scientists and researchers with the ability to communicate using computers, the Internet has grown rapidly over the past decade to include a diverse group of approximately 30 million users world-wide.

The Internet

Finally, we get to my favorite topic: multimedia living in the world-wide computer network known as the *Internet*.

Imagine having millions of CD-ROMs at your fingertips, without the need to swap them in and out of your computer. They are there, around the clock, just waiting for you to explore them. Every form of multimedia imaginable, and some things you'd never dream of, are all there for the taking. The *Internet*, or Cyberspace, as it is often called, is an electronic world residing on computer systems around the globe, all connected to one another.

Sound too good to be true? It almost is. But this is nothing new, mind you. Cyberspace has been around since World War II, originally developed by the U.S. Government to provide a way for scientists and scholars to communicate and exchange information using computers. Until recently, however, it was only available using text-based navigation, and we're not even talking about hypertext here. Originally there was no hypertext, pretty icons, or hypermedia to aid in communicating and navigating the Internet. But over the past few years, this massive world-wide computer network (formally known as the Internet) has become a hypermedia madhouse.

Today, *commercial on-line services* such as CompuServe, America Online, and Prodigy offer a friendly and easy-to-use gateway to the Internet. Hop on these services, and you'll find millions of other people just like yourself and millions more with whom you have nothing in common. Cyberspace is a world-wide network of people, connected through computers. And you can just imaging what bringing the world together in one giant meeting room would be like. The Internet is as close to civilized anarchy as you'll find today, and it is where the real revolution is taking place.

Once you have a connection to the Internet (either through a commercial on-line service or with a direct connection to the front lines where the hottest the action is found), you've become part of the revolution, willing or not. You become part of our world's only collective voice, and are free to explore the planet from the comfort of your computer. Every form of multimedia and standard information you could possible want is here: access to government documents, interactive multimedia games, magazines and books, reference guides, medical and legal databases, television broadcast schedules, music, photographs, movies, and virtual reality. And these are only a few of the things you'll find. Just the thought of all this information gathered together from around the world, instantly available to the world, brings tears to my eyes.

commercial on-line service Specialized on-line services provided by commercial companies such as America Online, Prodigy, and CompuServe. Commercial on-line services typically provide members with access to a multitude of software products, on-line discussion forums, technical support from a variety of vendors, and the ability to communicate using electronic mail (e-mail).

Perhaps the thought of all this doesn't seem terribly moving to you. Believe me, it is. Once you've had a taste of cyberspace you'll find that television loses its luster, books and magazines are put back on the shelf, and pepperoni pizza loses its flavor. All you'll want to do is sit in front of your computer with a steaming mug of fresh coffee and a nice blueberry muffin, exploring worlds you've never dreamed of.

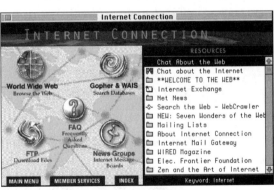

▶ *The fastest and most economical way to get connected to the vast Internet is through a commercial on-line service.*

And, personally, if I could navigate cyberspace with my toes while reclining on the couch, I'd never leave the house. Trust me, this is where it's at.

A Few Other Places

There are a multitude of other areas where multimedia is found, although these may not be quite as obvious or visible as those discussed above. Multimedia technology is beginning to appear in nearly every discipline known to man, and will soon become a fixture in every area where the need for presentation, communication, and learning exists. Following are just a few of the places where multimedia is now in use.

Architecture

Replacing the traditional, painstaking approach of drafting designs on trace paper and building miniature models to scale, specialized multimedia tools allow architects to rapidly test a variety of designs with unprecedented precision. Some products even offer "Virtual Walkthroughs," allowing architects and clients to enter a structure and walk around as if taking an actual tour. A similar approach is taken in the real estate industry, where prospective home owners can tour any number of homes without leaving their agent's office.

Government

From space shuttle launches to military combat simulators, our government has embraced multimedia. Using sophisticated technology, realistic simulations can be created that accurately depict their real-world counterparts. Although the cost of these simulators is extremely high and often requires the assistance of specially trained experts, enormous benefits are gained by the ability to test a multitude of "what if" scenarios instantly. What if certain parts of a space shuttle malfunctioned during a landing? What if a nuclear strike were begun by North Korea? What if our national deficit were reduced by a few billion dollars? All of these questions and many more can be simulated accurately using advanced multimedia technology.

Law Enforcement

Traditional police composite sketch artists are beginning to find the combination of computers and multimedia software an invaluable tool in re-creating the likeness of criminals, suspects, missing children, and also unidentifiable remains, not to mention animated crime scenes. In fact, a recent advance in the search for missing children was made possible through the combination of photographs and text in cyberspace, known as Living Desktop for Missing Children. This freely available tool distrib-

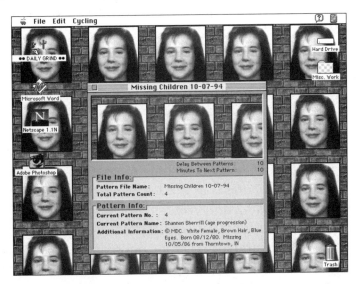

▶ *Mantis Development Corporation's* Living Desktop for Missing Children *is a public service version of the product and is available on-line free of charge. With the click of a button, users can view detailed information associated with any piece of Living Desktop artwork.*

utes through cyberspace the images and personal information (age, height, weight, eye color, and so on) of children missing in the United States. As a public service addition to law enforcement's crime-fighting effort, this tool and a similar product targeted at criminals combines multimedia with cyberspace for the benefit of everyone.

Medicine

Wouldn't you feel better if the doctor about to perform surgery on you had extensive experience in the procedure you require? And wouldn't you feel even more at ease if that surgeon could practice your very own surgery a few times before actually getting down to the nitty-gritty? Such is the case in many medical areas where, with the aid of virtual reality multimedia, surgeons can practice procedures as often as necessary without endangering the patient. In some cases, your own unique procedure can be simulated on the computer, without your body ever being touched. And when the time comes to slip into that breezy hospital gown and inhale the laughing gas, you'll be relieved to know your surgeon has already performed a few dozen trial runs without a hitch. Cut away, doc.

Music

Another utterly fascinating area where multimedia has been found is in the music industry, and I'm not just talking about the amazing visual effects found in every MTV video. Far from it. Today, musicians are beginning to play virtual instruments. Donning a pair of virtual reality video goggles and high technology data gloves, performers on the forefront of the music world can reach out to a variety of instruments that exist only in the computer, yet are played through speakers and similar broadcast systems with the full fidelity of the real thing. Not only available to serious musicians, multimedia products such as *Virtual Guitar* teach budding virtuosos how to play a specific instrument while allowing them to play side by side with music industry greats, such as rock and rollers Aerosmith. My, how times have changed.

PART 3

What Makes Up a Multimedia Computer?

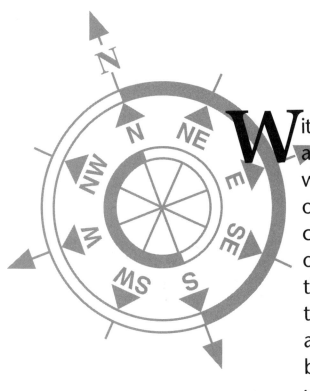

With multimedia all around us, how do we get into the thick of it ourselves? You could get your hands on multimedia through a home entertainment system or an information kiosk, but these both offer very narrow multimedia experiences. Your best bet is a properly configured personal computer, which can deliver nearly every type of multimedia imaginable. Why is this?

Basic Requirements for Multimedia

It all boils down to computing power. Information kiosks are designed for public access to a very specific form of information; you get only what they offer. Don't even think about using an information kiosk to experience a variety of multimedia titles; it simply doesn't have the power or equipment necessary to provide anything more than basic information navigation. The same is true for home entertainment systems such as Nintendo, Sega, and Atari. These devices focus exclusively on entertainment and have all the power necessary to deliver high quality multimedia games but not much more. And as you now know, there is a world of multimedia out there waiting to be explored. If you want to get your hands on the hottest multimedia available today, you'll do it using a multimedia computer.

What's a Multimedia Computer?

Multimedia computer? Aren't all computers multimedia devices to begin with? Absolutely not. You'll find yourself in a world of disappointment, not multimedia, if you aren't careful when buying a computer. Many computers are designed for basic tasks such as word processing and spreadsheets, and can't even begin to hint at a multimedia experience. If you are in the market for a new multimedia computer, or simply want to upgrade your existing machine to provide a decent multimedia experience, there are a few things you should know before you plunk down a fistful of dollars.

First, you must become comfortable with the various pieces of equipment that make up a multimedia computer. The requirements for a multimedia computer are essentially the same, regardless of who makes it. But before memorizing a list of equipment requirements or ripping the pages out of this book for reference, think for a moment about the nature of multimedia itself. What can you expect with any given multimedia product? Understanding the nature of multimedia makes it much easier to understand the equipment required to experience multimedia, and in the end it all makes sense.

The Nature of Multimedia

We know that multimedia is the combination of two or more media types: video, photographs, animation, text, sound, and/or music combined in a way you can control to some degree. Each medium is either seen or heard. So to truly experience multimedia, we must be able to see and hear the contents while exercising control over them.

We also know that it takes a great amount of human effort to create a multimedia product, which translates directly into a great deal of computing power required to experience the final result. Because of the very nature of multimedia, there must be a means to see, hear, and interact with the contents of a

▶ A multimedia computer must be powerful enough to provide interaction with any combination of video, photographs, animation, text, sound, and music. (from Brøderbund's Where in the World Is Carmen Sandiego?)

multimedia product. For our purposes, the very least you'll need to experience multimedia is a computer system powerful enough to provide interaction with any combination of video, photographs, animation, text, sound, and music. When you have a computer that provides these capabilities, you have, in essence, a multimedia computer.

To fully express the nature of multimedia, a computer system must possess three distinct capabilities: video display, audio play-back, and the raw computing power necessary to deliver it all while providing interactivity. Without each of these capabilities, you can't have a multimedia computer. When properly assembled, however, the result is an incredible computer system capable of providing the best experience multimedia has to offer. Finding and assembling the various components of a multimedia system can be quite a challenge, as well as expensive. Before looking at the bottom line, let's first take a look at each of these components in more detail.

▶ The requirements for an adequate multimedia computer are no mystery, and once assembled, will bring you hours of enjoyment. (from Creative Multimedia's Who Killed Sam Rupert?)

Video Display (Monitor)

The *video display,* or *monitor,* is the part of a computer system that looks very much like a television screen. While the guts of the system are hidden away inside a steel and plastic box, the monitor is our window into the secret world of the computer. Through the monitor we are able to see what is going on, to view the action. Without a monitor, most computers would be worthless, just as television broadcast signals are worthless to us without a television set. If you can't see it, you can't use it. Period.

video display (monitor) The video display, or monitor, is the part of a computer system that looks like a television screen and allows you to see what is going on inside. Without a monitor, you wouldn't be able to use your computer or see any portion of a multimedia product.

Only a handful of years ago, before the multimedia revolution began to take shape, the average computer system was used only to display text and the occasional graphic image. Moving video wasn't even a consideration in those dark ages of computing, and the typical video display system was a reflection of that fact. For the most part, graphic images were viewed only on computers reserved for very special purposes. Back then, the ability to display graphics was very expensive and available only for specialized uses such as graphic design, architecture, publishing, and advertising. The rest of us slugged along with *low-resolution,* black-and-white video displays, since the majority of our computer usage revolved around text — plain old text, the stuff you are reading this very moment. We had no need for high-resolution, full-color video displays. Until now.

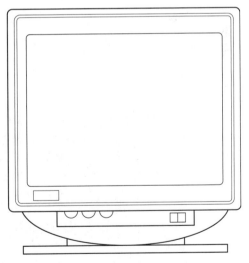

▶ *The video monitor, or display, is your window into the inside world of your computer.*

resolution Technically speaking, resolution is defined by the number of picture elements, or pixels, available for display. Resolution is generally spoken of in terms of width and height, such as 640 x 480 (640 pixels wide by 480 pixels high). The more pixels, the higher the resolution of a device or image.

video card The equipment that makes it possible for a video display to work properly. Tucked away inside the computer itself, this card, or board, transfers the visual contents of your computer to the monitor for your viewing pleasure.

Most entry-level computer systems sold today offer higher quality video displays than were available only a few years ago. Thanks to rapid advances in technology spurred by the emergence of multimedia and ravenous consumer demand, the cost of high resolution, full-color video displays has dropped considerably while their overall quality has risen. Although this is great from a consumer standpoint, these same factors have created an overabundance of choices when shopping for a video system. Picking the best monitor for your multimedia system isn't as easy as you might hope. For assistance in choosing the right monitor for your system, refer to Appendix A. For another piece of the multimedia puzzle, read on.

Video Card

What's this? More video equipment? But of course. While the video monitor is your window into the soul of the computer, there is an additional piece of equipment that must be in place before the techno-seance can begin: the *video card*. Tucked away inside the computer itself there must reside an interface card that transfers the visual contents of your computer to the monitor for your viewing pleasure. Think of it as a high-tech antenna for your computer. Without a video card, the monitor will stare blankly back at you since there is no way for the images and text inside the computer to be displayed.

Every computer display requires a video card, and multimedia systems must have a display and card combination capable of transferring text and color images very rapidly. It's simply not enough to have any combination of monitor and video card; both must be designed with multimedia in mind. This means that both the display and the card must support color, and the card must be able to process the image data quickly and then pass the information to the monitor without a noticeable delay. Anything less will result in choppy video playback and a sluggish, disappointing performance whenever color images are displayed.

High speed memory is an important part of any video card and comes built directly onto the card itself. This memory, video *random access memory* (*RAM*), or simply video RAM, is the lightning-fast storage where images reside before they are transferred to the video display. Generally speaking, the more video RAM a card has, the more colors it can display and the faster it will perform. Most multimedia video cards come with one megabyte (1MB) or more of video RAM built onto the card. If a video card doesn't have enough video RAM to hold an image or series of images, it may steal storage space from standard RAM. The result is a loss in an overall performance, and can be avoided by ensuring at least 1MB of video RAM is available directly on your video card.

And, just as there is a plethora of video monitors to choose from, there are even more video cards to wade through. Some computers even come with a built-in video card as part of the system. These *on-board video cards* are quite convenient, since you only have to plug the monitor in and you're up and running. Without on-board video, you must choose the right video card for your system and then install it yourself or, better yet, have someone else install it.

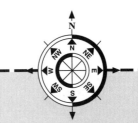

random access memory (RAM) The high speed memory, or storage, essential for fast interaction with the computer and software products.

on-board video card Some computers come with a built-in, or on-board, video card as part of the system. These on-board video cards are quite convenient, since you only have to plug in the monitor and you're up and running.

▶ *Computer devices, such as the video display and audio speakers, require that a compatible card be installed before they can be used. Some cards come preinstalled, while others must be installed manually.*

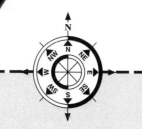

bundles Two or more products sold together, rather than individually, usually at a price lower than what you would pay if you purchased each product separately. Software bundles are a group of software products gathered together and sold as a single product. Hardware bundles are also common, typically bundled with a number of software products to make the deal more attractive.

Given all the options and potential confusion that can arise when shopping for the right video monitor and video card, you're probably best off buying a package deal that combines a video display and matching video card. Not only do these *bundles* include all the equipment you'll need, they are often cheaper than buying each piece individually. Many bundles include the entire multimedia computer, making it that much easier to get into multimedia. And to make the deal even sweeter, many bundles come preinstalled so you don't have to worry about ripping open and fiddling with a mess of delicate computer innards. As icing on the cake, free multimedia products are often tossed in the bundle so you're up and experiencing multimedia from the very start.

Bundles can be quite a deal, and are also available for those folks who already own a computer but want to add the necessary equipment to make their system multimedia capable. *Upgrade kits* can also be a great deal; they are discussed in more detail in Part 4.

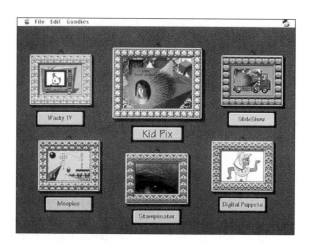

▶ *A diverse selection of excellent multimedia titles often comes as part of a multimedia bundle. (from Brøderbund's* Kid Pix Studio)

For the time being, you must simply understand that a video card must accompany a video display. Without it, even the best monitor in the world can't show you what is going on inside your computer. Whether purchased separately, as part of a pre-packaged bundle, or available directly onboard the computer, a video card must be present before you'll see anything at all. To add yet another step to the video tango, you must be certain that your video card and video display are compatible. Just any old video card won't do — you must ensure that the card and board are compatible. Luckily, any salesperson or computer company worth its salt can help you find the perfect match.

Which leads me to an important point when shopping around: don't for a moment consider paying for a piece of computer equipment (video display, video card, or any other component) without the care and attention of a knowledgeable and patient salesperson. You wouldn't buy a car or major appliance without reasonable assistance and advice, and your computer purchases should be no different. Today, technical support and customer service are as important as the computer product itself. Without top-notch service and support behind you, choosing, buying, assembling, and using your "dream team" of multimedia equipment can quickly turn into a real-life nightmare. Don't chance it.

upgrade kits Multimedia hardware bundles that feature the necessary equipment to make an existing computer system multimedia capable. These upgrade kits typically include a sound card and speakers, CD-ROM drive, and a number of multimedia titles.

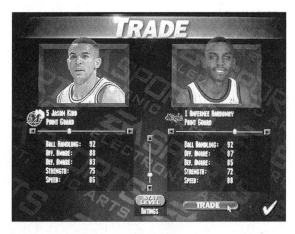

▶ A "dream team" of multimedia equipment is not essential, but you should shop around to make sure you find the right equipment for your own needs. (from Electronic Arts Sports Basketball)

audio card (sound card) The equipment that makes it possible for computerized sound to be played on speakers. Just as the video activity going on inside a multimedia computer requires a video display and video card to be seen, both an audio card and speakers are required for sound to be heard.

Audio Card (Sound Card) and Speakers

Another card?! I'm afraid so, but this time it isn't for video, but sound. Just as there is a world of video activity going on inside a multimedia computer that requires a video display and video card to be seen, there is an audio side to the equation that requires both an *audio (or sound) card* and speakers to be heard.

The audio card is responsible for creating and playing sounds that are ultimately heard through the speakers, and so it is important that your sound card be capable of producing high quality audio. Sound quality is measured as "bits of resolution," indicating how many different levels of acoustic energy are produced. The higher the resolution, the better the quality of sound. An 8-bit resolution sound has 256 levels of acoustic energy, while a 16-bit resolution sound has over 16,000 levels. The very highest resolution sounds, 32-bit, have over 24 million levels and produce the highest level of audio possible. In order to hear these sounds, your system must have a card capable of reading high-resolution sounds.

At a minimum, look for a card with 8-bit capability, although 16-bit is better. For the ultimate sound quality, invest in a 32-bit sound card. While it is possible to play low-resolution sounds on a high-resolution card (i.e., playing an 8-bit sound on a 16-bit card), you cannot go the

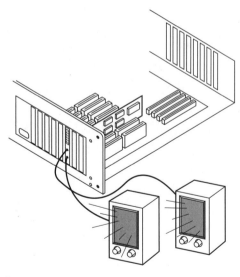

▶ *The device card is installed inside the computer, after which the device itself is attached to it. Shown here is an installed audio card that has been attached to a pair of multimedia speakers.*

other direction. If you have a low-resolution card, it can only play low-resolution sounds. Save yourself the hassle and invest in at least a 16-bit sound card.

Also be certain your audio card comes with the *MIDI (Musical Instrument Digital Interface)* format. MIDI makes it possible for your system to play sounds and music in this special format. The MIDI format is different from other computer sound formats in that it is more similar to sheet music than an actual recording. MIDI doesn't merely play back the recording of an audio source. Instead, MIDI sounds are composed of individual instruments, each having its own responsibility. When played, each instrument in a MIDI sound is individually activated, resulting in audio being generated as an orchestra would play sheet music as opposed to simply playing back an audio recording. Although not all multimedia titles contain sound in the MIDI format, this feature is common to most audio cards and should be present on yours.

Although your computer already has a speaker built into it, the majority of multimedia titles include rich audio material that can't be heard through these puny things. Why, then, do computer makers bother with these built-in speakers in the first place if we have to go out and spend more cash to hear the world of multimedia? The answer lies in the way various sounds are stored and played on computers.

Basic sounds such as the "beep" or "buzz" you hear when the computer wants your attention are fairly primitive and can be played over the tiny built-in speaker quite easily. Although more complex sounds such as speech and music can often be played through a built-in speaker, the sound quality is ruined because these units simply can't deliver the richness and volume required.

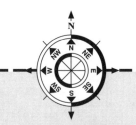

MIDI (Musical Instrument Digital Interface) Specialized music technology, typically a combination of specialized hardware and software, that provides the ability to record and/or play back musical instruments using the computer. MIDI music is very different from computerized digital audio sources: digital audio is an actual recording of music, whereas MIDI is similar to sheet music that is used to command different musical instruments which, when played together, generate the final audio sound.

CD-ROM drive A device that makes it possible for your computer to use CD-ROMs, a variation of the audio CD. A single CD-ROM holds the equivalent of nearly 600 low-capacity floppy disks and typically contains graphics, sound, and/or text. The CD-ROM drive gives your computer access to the information found on CD-ROMs.

The built-in speaker is fine for basic computer sounds, but multimedia can provide full-blown stereo sound at the same quality found on audio compact discs. Try to play this at full-tilt through the built-in speaker and it may be destroyed altogether. In order to experience the full fidelity of multimedia sound you must install both an audio card and a pair of quality speakers.

You wouldn't be satisfied with an 8-track tape player in an otherwise fully equipped sports car, so why compromise the quality of your multimedia experience by limping along with your computer's built-in speaker? Even if you decide against investing in an audio card and speakers, most multimedia products on the market today simply won't play through the built-in speaker. You won't hear a thing, except perhaps the "beep" or "buzz" of the computer trying to get your attention when it tells you it can't play the audio portion of a product because a valid sound system isn't installed!

Not to worry, many multimedia bundles also throw in the audio card and a pair of decent speakers for good measure. You don't have to hunt around for the perfect card and matching speakers, unless you enjoy the challenge. Simply evaluate the contents of any multimedia bundle or upgrade package with a keen eye, as explained in the following chapter and Appendix A, and you'll be well on your way to a glorious multimedia experience.

CD-ROM Drive

Wait a minute! Where does a *CD-ROM drive* come into play? After all, as long as the video and audio parts are up to snuff, all that remains for a multimedia computer is the computer itself, right?

Right. Once you have a powerful-enough computer attached to an equally capable video card and monitor, and also have the necessary sound board and speakers attached, you have what amounts to a multimedia computer. But, on the whole, you'd be missing the multimedia boat if you didn't include a CD-ROM drive.

Technically speaking, you would have the absolute essentials required to provide a true multimedia experience: computing power, video and audio, plus the ability to interact with the contents. Ahhh . . . the contents. While you'd have the tools necessary to use multimedia, you must somehow gain access to multimedia products. And the most popular way of getting your hands on personal computer multimedia products is through CD-ROM. No matter how powerful your computer or how slick your audio and video system, you need a way to get to the multimedia. Without a CD-ROM drive, your souped-up computer system is much like a car without tires.

Sure, you can do donuts in the driveway or tear up the lawn terrorizing stray cats and squirrels, but you're really dying to get on the road and unleash the full potential of your new pride and joy. Like a candy-apple red sports car without the open road, a multimedia computer without a CD-ROM drive is a very, very sad sight. All that power and promise, with nowhere to go and nothing to see.

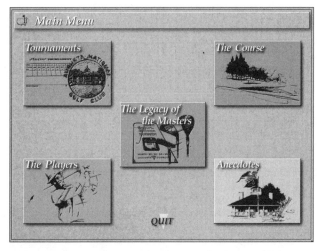

▶ *With a fully equipped multimedia computer, traditional outdoor activities can be pursued indoors anytime. (from Creative Multimedia's* The Masters)

How about using the floppy diskette drive that comes with every computer? Here's a way to get access to multimedia, right? It certainly is, and it's guaranteed to drive you insane in the process. Remember, a single CD-ROM holds the equivalent of nearly 600 low-capacity floppy disks. Try shuffling 600 or so of these things in and out of your computer as you try to keep focused on the multimedia experience at hand. Forget it.

As a matter of fact, the vast majority of CD-ROM products come only on CD-ROM. Manufacturers aren't about to waste a pile of cash spreading their multimedia products over hundreds of floppy disks when the CD-ROM format is cheaper to begin with. And if it makes the decision any easier, most CD-ROM drives provide the ability to play standard audio CDs as well. With these you'll get all the benefits of CD-ROM, and be able to pop in your favorite audio CDs for a musical fiesta whenever you like, all without leaving the comfort of your computer. Face it, you need a CD-ROM drive. The real question is, what speed?

The Need for Speed

Today's CD-ROM drives come in a variety of speeds. The speed of a CD-ROM drive is a measure of how fast it can get information from the surface of a CD-ROM to you. This is also known as the

▶ *Without a CD-ROM drive, your multimedia computer is like a sports car without tires: full of promise and power, but no way to get going.*

data transfer rate. When CD-ROM drives first appeared on the scene, the term "speed" wasn't used to describe transfer rate. Back then, you had to understand more cryptic terms such as "sustained transfer rate," "data seek time," and "platter revolutions per second," which, when taken all together, gave the overall speed of a drive. Over the past few years, faster and more capable CD-ROM drives have arrived on the scene, along with the term *speed* to describe their data transfer rate, which help consumers get a rough idea of a drive's capabilities without getting lost in the mire of technical terminology. And for this we are thankful.

speed (data transfer rate) A measure of how fast a CD-ROM drive can get information from the surface of a CD-ROM to you. Currently there are four different speeds to choose from when evaluating CD-ROM drives: single (1x), double (2x), triple (3x), and quadruple (4x). Single-speed drives are the slowest, and quadruple-speed drives are the fastest.

At this point there are basically four different speeds to choose from when evaluating CD-ROM drives: single (1x), double (2x), triple (3x), and quadruple (4x). Many manufacturers and advertisers use the shorthand notation rather than the actual word when describing CD-ROM drive speeds, and so it isn't unusual to see a double-speed drive advertised as "2x" or a quadruple-speed as "4x." These shorthand notations are easy to recognize while conserving valuable space on product packaging and advertisements. And, since brief descriptions like "3x" and "4x" take up considerably less ink than the phrases "triple speed" and "quadruple," more space on the product's packaging and advertisements can be dedicated to snazzy images and juicy customer testimonials.

When it comes to performance, the slowest drives in the bunch are, of course, single speed (1x). The original CD-ROM drives to hit the stores were single speed and have since nearly disappeared from the marketplace altogether. Today's standard is the double-speed drive (2x), which is twice as fast as the single speed. Triple-speed (3x) drives are even faster, delivering three times the performance of the original single-speed drive. But the undisputed champ of

CD-ROM drives is, at least for the moment, quadruple speed (*quad-speed*, or 4x). Quad-speed drives perform four times as fast as their original single-speed ancestors and give the best all-around performance out of the bunch. Will quad-speed drives remain at the top? Nope.

Although rip-roaring when compared to 1x drives, quad-speed drives won't remain king of the hill for long. Already beginning to sneak onto store shelves are 6x drives, and new technology breakthroughs continue to drive the price of CD-ROM drives down while performance and capacity increase. There is really only one thing you can depend on in the computer industry: by the time you decide on a product, pay for it, and bring it home, a stronger, faster, and cheaper version will be announced. Count on it.

▶ CD-ROM drives come in a variety of speeds, from the sleepy single speed (1x) drive to the blazing quadruple speed (4x) units. Even faster drives are now making their way to store shelves, promising to make today's 4x drives slow by comparison.

Choosing a Speed

So what's the best buy if things are always changing? There is no right answer to this question when talking about CD-ROM drives or any other computer product, for that matter. You must take into consideration your budget, your basic requirements for the product in question, and how much you actually need or want the product. These things must each be considered and carefully balanced in order to make a solid choice. It's clear that a CD-ROM drive is a must when assembling any multimedia computer, and so the real questions are "How much can I afford to spend?" and "What speed do I need?"

But be careful. You'll be plenty sorry if you buy a new CD-ROM drive based on price and speed alone. And while the original cryptic terms used to measure the various capabilities of CD-ROM drives are still around today, only the brave of heart dare to compare drives based on these measurements alone when hunting for the best buy. The rest of us are better off letting the industry magazines test and rank the variety of drives now on the market, in the end telling us in writing where to find the best bang for the buck.

quad-speed CD-ROM drive The undisputed champ of CD-ROM drives is, at least for the moment, quadruple speed (quad-speed or 4x). Quad-speed drives perform four times as fast as their original single-speed ancestors and give the best all-around performance out of the bunch. Drives faster than 4x are now beginning to appear on the market, although 2x (double speed) remains the industry standard because most multimedia products available today don't take advantage of higher speed drives.

Product testers who work for industry magazines and journals take the time to evaluate each drive in a real-world setting, where an extensive array of statistics printed on product packaging and advertisements mean nothing. Performance is what counts here, not a flashy package or an impressive list of statistics. Leave it to these professionals to do the research for you; it's what they do best. You'll soon find all the performance numbers printed on the side of a box are essentially meaningless; what's important is real-world performance, reliability, and the recommendation of a professional who has used the product. No vendor in his or her right mind is going to let you take home an armful of new drives for free to help figure out which one is best for you.

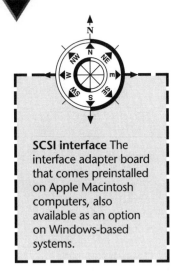

SCSI interface The interface adapter board that comes preinstalled on Apple Macintosh computers, also available as an option on Windows-based systems.

Product testers also take the time to describe how a particular CD-ROM drive will connect to your system. Although many CD-ROM drives can be connected directly to the audio board, others require special interface boards that must be installed separately. The most common of these are the *Small Computer System Interface* (SCSI, pronounced "scuzzy") and IDE interface. While I recommend SCSI for its ease of use and ability to connect up to seven devices (CD-ROM drives, hard drives, scanners, and other hardware) using a single interface card, product testers describe the nuts and bolts of each option to help you make a decision based on your own needs.

Most important of all, you simply won't know how well a CD-ROM drive performs until you pay for it in advance, take it home, and spend the next few hours installing and tinkering with it. Stick with the recommendation of a professional. I suggest taking a peek inside *PC World, Macworld,* or *Byte* magazines whenever you need advice concerning the purchase of a piece of computer equipment, although there are a number of great industry journals to choose from. If what you are looking for can't be found in the current issue, give the magazine's main office a call and ask for any back issues that review the product you have in mind. In the end you won't be sorry; you'll save yourself time, money, and a great deal of aggravation.

Choosing an Operating System

At the heart of any multimedia system lies the computer. Whether for an information kiosk, a home entertainment system, or a personal computer system, computing power is the fundamental ingredient in any recipe for multimedia. The amount of computing power required for a true multimedia experience varies greatly and relates directly to the multimedia product itself. While an information kiosk and home entertainment system require very little in the way of computing power, they also provide a lesser degree of multimedia. If you want to experience the highest degree of multimedia possible, however, you'll need a powerful computer to do it.

Deciding which multimedia computer is best for you can be even more confusing than shopping for multimedia products. There is a wide range to choose from, with more options and add-ons than you can imagine. Luckily, there are standards that must be met for a computer to be considered capable of delivering a worthwhile multimedia experience. Before jumping into standards, let's first get familiar with the most popular multimedia computers out there.

Macintosh versus Windows

The majority of multimedia computers on the market are divided into two camps: those that run the Apple Macintosh operating system and those that run Microsoft Windows. Windows is not an operating system itself; it is actually a software product that runs on top of the DOS operating system. Windows is, however, a graphical interface similar to the Macintosh operating system and is what most people will use when navigating their computer. DOS sits underneath Windows and performs all operating system functions required by Windows. For the purposes of this book, any reference to the Microsoft Windows operating system, or simply Windows, is meant to describe the combination of the Windows software interface and DOS. The exception is Windows 95, which is a true operating system having no reliance on DOS, described in detail below.

An *operating system* is the software that makes it possible to use a computer. The operating system is your interface for working with the various components of a computer, such as disk drives, monitors,

operating system The software that makes it possible to use a computer. The operating system is your interface for working with the various components of a computer, such as disk drives, monitors, hard disks, and filing systems. Without an operating system, a computer is just a box of expensive hardware that can't be used. Before the introduction of the graphically based Apple Macintosh, text-based operating systems were used.

hard disks, and filing systems. Without an operating system, a computer is just a box of expensive hardware that can't be used. Microsoft Windows, which runs over the DOS operating system, and Apple Macintosh are the most popular for multimedia personal computer operating systems. There are many other operating systems to choose from, such as OS/2, UNIX, and VMS, although this book is specifically focused on using Microsoft Windows and Apple Macintosh computers for multimedia purposes.

Confused? Think of a multimedia computer as a sports car. The guts of it, the hardware, are under the hood. The video display would be the windows and windshield; a way to view the world while driving. A stereo and decent speakers are needed, of course, so you can blare your favorite tunes as you tear up the road. Now, imagine all this but without a steering wheel, gas or brake pedals, or gear shift. These are the things that let you actually drive the car, the operating system if you will. Without these essentials, you're going nowhere. Of course we take these parts of the car for granted, expecting them to be there when we hop into the driver's seat, just as we often overlook the operating system that lets us take the computer for a spin.

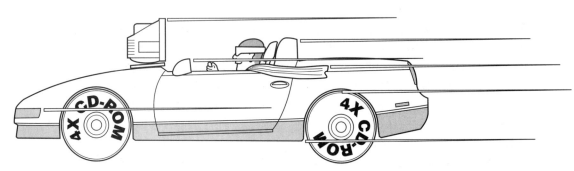

▶ *Generally speaking, the faster each device in your multimedia system is, the faster your system will perform overall. Although the double speed (2x) CD-ROM drive is the industry standard today, top-of-the-line quadruple speed (4x) units give an extra boost of performance to those with the need for speed.*

Without solid advice, however, choosing the right computer and operating system can be more difficult than buying a new car. There are just as many options to consider, and your best defense against making the wrong decision is knowledge. Read on.

Apple Macintosh

During Super Bowl XVIII in 1984, a small company by the name of Apple Computer televised the now-famous commercial that promised to change the world of personal computing. At that point in computing history, if you were using a computer you were part of a fairly elite crowd. Back then, there was no concept of a graphical operating system. To do even the most basic functions on a computer, you had to type in a number of cryptic commands using a keyboard. There was no mouse to point and click your way around; everything was based on text. Instead of clicking on an icon to run a program, you typed in something like **run a: PROGRAM**, followed by the Return key. To view the contents of a directory, the place where computer files are stored, you couldn't simply click on the picture of a folder. Here you would type something like **cd GAMES**, followed by the Return key and **directory more**, followed by the Return key. There was no room for error or misspelled words. Even the spaces had to be in exactly the right place to get anything done. Oh, it was some fun.

In 1984, Apple Computer introduced the Macintosh, "a computer for the rest of us," and the world of personal computing was forever changed. This adorable little box, which looked somewhat like a rectangular, beige hobbit crouching on the desk, ushered in an entirely new way of interacting with the computer. Gone were the

▶ *America Online, a popular commercial on-line service, is available for both Apple Macintosh systems and Windows-based systems.*

mouse A small plastic device attached to the computer by a thin cable through which it communicates with the operating system. Movements of the mouse are translated into movements of a pointer on the computer screen, which in turn is used to navigate the computer.

graphical operating system An operating system that relies heavily on graphic images and the use of a mouse to operate a computer.

days of typing esoteric commands, hunting and pecking at the keyboard with a stack of reference manuals at your side. Every Macintosh came tethered to a bizarre creature that revolutionized the way we navigated computers. Attached by a thin wire to the backside of every Macintosh was a *mouse*. This plastic rodent was not much larger than a pack of cigarettes, but it was every bit as potent.

Using the mouse to maneuver an arrow on the Macintosh video display (which was built into the computer itself, by the way), anyone could navigate the contents of this machine. Where once we were required to read cryptic text and type even more cryptic commands into the computer just to get around, the Apple Macintosh was entirely devoted to graphics and encouraged navigation. File directories looked like little manila folders, documents looked like miniature pads of paper, and application programs were easily identified by their triangular shape. To open or run any of these items, you simply used your mouse to position the arrow on top of the item, and then quickly clicked on the mouse button twice. Once an application or document was open, all of its associated commands were graphically available through menus. Instead of memorizing all the commands required for each program or document, you simply navigated through the menus using the mouse until you found what you were looking for. Sound familiar?

Breaking away from the text-based operating systems of its time, Apple revolutionized the way people interacted with the computer. No longer the exclusive domain of techies, whiz-kids, and business people, the Macintosh brought personal computers to the masses. And although the graphical operating system and mouse were not invented by Apple itself, but by scientists at the Xerox Palo Alto Research Center (Xerox PARC), it was Apple that saw their potential and moved them out of the labs and into our homes. We now take for granted the mouse and *graphical operating system,* which today are an integral part of nearly every personal computer in use. Thanks, folks.

Until recently, the only way to use the *Apple Macintosh operating system* was through an Apple Macintosh computer. The two went hand in hand. The Macintosh operating system was available only on Macintosh computers, unlike other operating systems that could be used on a variety of computer systems. Apple knew it had a good thing and refused to let other computer manufacturers in on it. Rather than allowing its operating system to be used on non-Macintosh computers, Apple preferred to sue the pants off anybody who dared to touch its crown jewel. Until this year, that is.

Realizing that it has been slowly starving itself of potential revenue all these years, Apple has recently begun to license the Macintosh operating system to other computer vendors. Soon you're likely to see all sorts of computers sporting the Macintosh operating system label, adding yet another level of complexity to the task of finding the right computer for your needs. Until these new systems are thoroughly re-viewed in industry magazines, you're better off buy-ing a real Macintosh than trying to save a few bucks buying a *clone.*

Until recently, the heart of every Macintosh was a *central process-ing unit* (*CPU*) computer chip designed by Motorola Corporation. A computer's CPU is the equivalent of a car's engine. It provides the raw power on which all other parts rely. While there are many facets to a computer, the CPU is usually considered the heart of any system. The heart of the first Macintosh to roll off the assembly line

Apple Macintosh operating system The graphically oriented operating system used with Apple Macintosh computers. Apple revolutionized the way people interacted with the computer when it introduced the first commercially available graphical operating system, breaking away from the text-based operating systems of its time.

clone A computer that looks and acts like a name-brand system, yet is not manufactured by the same company. You can often get the same or better performance from a clone than you would with a name-brand system, and you'll save a few dollars in the process.

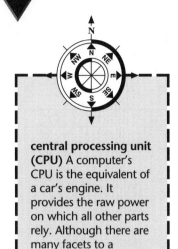

central processing unit (CPU) A computer's CPU is the equivalent of a car's engine. It provides the raw power on which all other parts rely. Although there are many facets to a computer, the CPU is usually considered the heart of any system.

was the Motorola 68000 CPU. Apple chose the Motorola 68000 CPU to power its original Macintosh computer, and stuck with that line of processors as it evolved.

Following the 68000, Motorola's 68020 CPU was promptly used in Apple's then-top-of-the-line system, the Macintosh II. As this series of Motorola chips advanced, it provided more raw computing power for the Macintosh computer and operating system to draw upon. Until recently, these chips were the heart of every Apple Macintosh. Beginning with the original 68000 and advancing through the 68020, 68030, and now the 68040, these CPUs have served the Macintosh well. But, eventually even good things come to an end.

In an effort to keep up with the demands of modern computer users, particularly the multimedia masses, Apple recently abandoned the Motorola 68000 line of CPUs in favor of the newly developed PowerPC CPU. Jointly developed by Motorola, IBM, and Apple, the PowerPC packs such a wallop you won't be sad to see the 68000 line of chips fade away. But none of this information really helps you decide on which multimedia Mac to buy, does it?

While perhaps not immediately useful, knowing the history behind the Macintosh and Apple's recent move from old to new CPU technology will help make sense of the growing marketplace, particularly when non-Apple computers running the Macintosh operating system begin to hit the shelves. In addition, you will now understand what I mean when I say, "While you may be able to experience multimedia with a 68020 Macintosh, I would recommend at least a 68030 Macintosh for solid performance. And if you're looking for the ultimate multimedia system, consider the PowerPC Macintoshes. They're more expensive, but offer over ten times the performance of their 680x0 relatives. If you're determined to build the best multimedia system possible, don't skimp on raw processing power. Go with PowerPC."

Microsoft Windows

On the flip side of the operating system coin sits Microsoft Windows, whose genesis and history is every bit as important and interesting as that of the Macintosh. Long before the Macintosh was introduced, even before the age of a personal computer industry dominated by the omnipotent International Business Machines (IBM), there was the humble beginning of today's largest and most powerful software company, Microsoft Corporation.

Eons ago in technology history, in the early 1970s, personal computers were nothing more than the bubbling imaginations of scientists and technology hobbyists enchanted and driven by the promise of miniaturized computers. At that point, the smallest computers were roughly the size of a large refrigerator and required just as much coolant to keep their innards running smoothly without overheating. A computer that working people could afford and that could fit easily on a desk was nothing more than a dream at the time. However, this dream was destined to become a reality, not by the profit-driven research and development teams of powerful computer companies of the day, but by the passionate commitment of a hobbyist named Ed Roberts and software developed by a young Harvard dropout and his teenage friend — Bill Gates and Paul Allen.

In 1975, the Altair computer marked the beginning of a new era in computing: personal computing. Built from scratch by Roberts in an Albuquerque, New Mexico, garage and driven by a makeshift operating system written by Gates and Allen in Cambridge, Massachusetts, the Altair was the first computer of its kind. Powered by the innovative 8080 CPU developed by Intel, the Altair was on the cutting edge of technology. Available only as a kit, new owners of the $400 wonder had to assemble the Altair themselves. There was no keyboard, let alone mouse, and no video display.

To complicate matters, there was no operating system as we know them today. In order to communicate with the Altair, users were required to enter computer instructions directly into the machine using a series of flip-switches on the front panel, rather like communicating in Morse code. Feedback came not as a line of text or graphics, but as a series of flashing lights since there was no video display. This was the dawn of a new era, and although terribly primitive by today's standards, it was a quantum leap forward in technology. No longer the exclusive domain of researchers and scientists who could afford the manpower and real estate required

▶ *Before the age of personal computers, large rooms were needed to house enormous mainframe computers that required constant cooling, very low room temperatures, and a number of attendants to keep them running smoothly.*

to maintain systems the size of pickup trucks, the computer had finally come into the home and onto the desk. The personal computer was born.

Although the be-all-end-all to hobbyists and technology buffs, the Altair was just the beginning for Gates and Allen. The company they founded in 1975, Microsoft, would eventually provide the operating system for personal computers around the world. And eventually, their ubiquitous text-oriented *Disk Operating System (DOS)* would provide the groundwork for their mouse-driven, graphical operating system called *Microsoft Windows.*

Although Microsoft Windows was initially a dismal failure when compared to the intuitive and personable Macintosh operating system, it posed enough of a threat to Apple Computer that the company eventually filed a copyright infringement lawsuit in 1988, claiming that Microsoft had violated an agreement the two companies had entered into in 1985. In this agreement, Microsoft acknowledged the proprietary nature of the Macintosh *graphical user interface (GUI),* to which it was granted a limited license for the purpose of developing software products for the Macintosh.

disk operating system (DOS) A text-oriented operating system developed by Microsoft that provided the groundwork for its mouse-driven, graphical operating system, Microsoft Windows.

Microsoft Windows operating system A graphically oriented computer operating system developed by Microsoft Corporation. Designed for use on systems powered by the Intel line of central processing units (CPUs), Microsoft Windows makes it possible to visually navigate these computers.

The two companies were initially allies while also spirited competitors in the burgeoning personal computer industry, but this first shot fired in the operating system wars would forever split the industry into two distinct camps: the laid-back, casually attired Macintosh camp and the more business-oriented, pinstriped, and wing tip-wearing Windows camp.

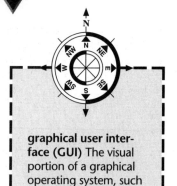

graphical user interface (GUI) The visual portion of a graphical operating system, such as windows, icons, menus, and the mouse pointer.

Choosing an operating system is often very personal, reflecting quite a bit about the users themselves; people take their operating system to heart and will defend its virtue valiantly against those who dare speak badly of it. To this very day the Macintosh versus Windows operating system war rages on in office buildings, classrooms, homefronts, and in higher courts across the nation, while the actual gap between Macintosh and Windows operating systems steadily narrows.

The newest version of Windows, Windows 95, promises to capture every ounce of elegance and power found in the Macintosh operating system while providing a host of its very own refinements and features. Doing away with its reliance on DOS altogether, Windows 95 is a full-fledged operating system. Designed from the onset with multimedia in mind, industry watchdogs and pundits herald Windows 95 as the operating system to beat all operating systems. And while the truth remains to be seen, for all the hype and industry buzz surrounding the long-delayed release, one thing is certain: Microsoft is betting the future on Windows 95.

Decisions, Decisions

What does this all mean for you? Will the ultimate multimedia machine come from Apple or Microsoft? While the rest of the computing world holds its breath for the answer, you're better off simply getting on with the show and getting into multimedia. And if you haven't already bought into a computer system, ask yourself the following question:

"Would I rather invest in the easiest multimedia machine to install and use, or in a more complex system that might turn my hair gray a little faster but will provide instant compatibility with the majority of personal computers around the world?"

If you are looking for the easiest machine to install and use, something you and the kids will have no problem mastering, then take a look at the Macintosh. On the other hand, if you would like to shuttle computer files between the office and home, or share them with friends, you'll likely be looking at a Windows machine. Either way, you'll have access to the vast majority of today's best multimedia titles, since most developers offer their products for both platforms.

▶ *Most popular multimedia products, such as Origin's* BioForge, *are available cross-platform (for Apple Macintosh and Microsoft Windows).*

A Few Standards To Live By

Having entirely avoided the topic of CPU and hardware requirements for Microsoft Windows computers, now is the time to dive in. Not surprisingly, Windows doesn't run on the Motorola line of CPUs. Just as in the days of the Altair, Microsoft's latest and greatest operating system is powered by Intel chips. And although the twilight of the 8080 has long passed and build-'em-yourself computer kits have faded from memory, a vibrant and powerful new line of Intel processors are blazing the path to multimedia enlightenment: Pentium.

Just as Apple chose the Motorola line of processors to power its Macintosh computers, Microsoft chose the line of Intel CPUs to provide the juice. Starting with the Intel 286, followed by the 386 and finally the 486, Microsoft Windows relied on the x86 line of CPUs to provide the power. But unlike Apple, Microsoft remains solely a software company; it doesn't make computers at all. This approach has served Microsoft very, very well. Currently the Windows operating system is used approximately 10 times more often than the Macintosh, with the slickest version of all, Windows 95, just out. Not too shabby for a few boys who kicked it all off a long time ago with the Altair.

While Microsoft and Apple go head-to-head in the battle for personal computer market share, Intel and Motorola face off in the great CPU war. Just as Motorola has evolved from the 680x0 line of CPUs to the PowerPC era, Intel has gone from the x86 series to a new chip altogether, the Pentium. Where Motorola has worked with both Apple and IBM to create its newest generation CPU, Intel has done it alone. The end result is a neck-and-neck race between CPU manufacturers every bit as intense and spirited as that between Apple and Microsoft.

Although this stiff competition results in more choices and potentially more confusion when shopping for a multimedia computer, it also means the savvy buyer walks away the winner. Cutthroat competition in the CPU and operating system worlds drives prices down while the quality skyrockets. And if you know what you're looking for, the deals can be tremendous. This is where standards come in handy.

Minimum Standards

Let's begin by looking at the minimum standards for today's entry-level multimedia system. At a minimum, the video system must support 256 different colors, and the audio system must pump out at least 8-bit mono sound, although 16,000 colors and 16-bit stereo sound will soon be the standard. For now, 256 colors and 8-bit mono sound are the absolute minimum video and audio requirements to look for, while a hefty amount of random access memory (RAM) and a large hard drive are just as important. RAM is the high speed memory essential for fast interaction with the computer and software products. A hard drive is used to permanently store the operating system and various files needed for multimedia and other programs.

RAM

Before any software product can run, multimedia or otherwise, it must be loaded from permanent storage, such as a hard drive or CD-ROM, into the high speed, temporary storage known as RAM. Permanent storage is where files normally reside, storage which goes undisturbed when the computer is restarted or the power is turned off. RAM, on the other hand, is volatile, temporary storage that is erased when the computer is restarted or the power is turned off. RAM, however, handles information at incredibly high speeds and is where software products must be located before they can be used. The process of transferring software from permanent storage into RAM is handled automatically by the operating system.

Once a program is in high speed RAM, the computer can perform its magic. Generally speaking, the more RAM a computer system has, the faster it will perform. If not enough RAM is available, some products can't be used at all. Each software product has its own unique RAM requirements, although at a minimum you'll need 8 megabytes (MB), regardless of what type of computer you have. Anything less and you're practically guaranteed ulcers. If possible, move up to 16 MB or more of RAM. You'll avoid a lot of memory-related problems while speeding up the system overall, and at the same time you'll be prepared for the most current, RAM-hungry multimedia titles.

CD-ROM Drive

When it comes to a CD-ROM drive, the current standard is double-speed (2x). This will change in time, although 2x drives are perfectly adequate for the majority of multimedia titles on the market today and will also accommodate most of the newest arrivals.

hard drive A device used to permanently store the operating system and various files needed for multimedia and other programs. A relatively slow form of storage, the hard drive is considerably faster than the CD-ROM drive yet much slower than high-speed RAM.

Quad-speed (4x) drives are also available, and prices are dropping rapidly, which makes them a reasonable consideration when compared to 2x drives. However, very few multimedia titles can take advantage of the speed of these fast drives, and most won't until there are enough units in the market to justify it. For the time being, you're better off buying a 2x drive and saving the money for extra RAM or hard-drive space.

Hard Drive

Although the majority of your multimedia titles will come on CD-ROM, most of these products copy some portion of their content onto your hard drive. This happens regardless of the operating system or system configuration. Since hard drives are much faster than CD-ROM drives, multimedia products will usually copy critical portions of their content to the hard drive to increase their overall speed. This is common among all titles, and so a large hard drive is essential for a multimedia system.

▶ In order to ride Origin's Wings of Glory, you will need a multimedia computer equipped with a CD-ROM drive.

If you purchase a system with less than 500 megabytes (MB) of hard drive space, at some point you'll probably need to manually remove outdated files from the drive to make room for more current multimedia titles. Save yourself the aggravation and invest in a 500 MB (or larger) hard drive. To prepare for upcoming multimedia titles, I would suggest a 1 gigabyte drive (1,000 MB, or "One Gig"). One Gig is an extremely large capacity drive, which may seem excessive. It will, however, accommodate a large number of the most demanding multimedia titles while leaving enough space for standard computer programs such as word processors, spreadsheets, databases, communications, and so on.

Operating System and CPU

As for the actual computer itself and which operating system to choose, there is no standard to help you make a decision. It ultimately comes down to what you expect to gain from the system, who you expect to exchange files with, and what you are most comfortable using. If you have experience with the Macintosh, you should probably stick with that system. The same goes for Windows.

Buying a computer is a major decision, not one to take lightly. Talk with friends and coworkers about their experiences, ask them for advice, and read a few industry reviews about both platforms to give you the unbiased facts. I can no better advise you on the type of computer system to buy than I can on the type of car you should drive. A lot of personal decisions go into the mix, each of which you must carefully consider and balance before making a choice. Regardless of which system you choose, however, there are standards for each when it comes to building a capable multimedia system.

Although I've discussed the basic standards for multimedia components, these standards, together with standards for both the Macintosh and Windows platform, are discussed in more detail in Appendix A. Regardless of your ultimate decision, you'll want the best system for your money. And thanks to massive competition in the operating system, CPU, and computer industry in general, it's easier than ever to walk out with a great bargain as long as you walk in armed with the knowledge of what makes up a multimedia computer and an understanding of the industry standards.

The Chicken and the Egg

As the power of personal computers increases, the quality of multimedia products grows accordingly. The very best multimedia titles always seem to require the most powerful computers on the market, creating a modern "chicken and the egg" scenario. Which comes first, better computers that spur the creation of better multimedia products, or do the best multimedia products create consumer demand for faster and less-expensive computers? The answer is, not surprisingly, a little of both.

Computer makers are constantly improving their technology, racing to the market with ever bigger and better systems to sell. Multimedia manufacturers use this state-of-the-art technology to create the best products they possibly can, knowing that in a short period of time these machines will come down in price and reach the mass market. The personal computer and multimedia product markets constantly push one another to higher levels, which is a good thing when it comes to creating new and innovative products, but it can cause a headache when it comes to buying a machine that won't be outdated the moment you walk out of the store. The next section of this book, Part 4, will lead you through the maze of multimedia options and take some of the pain out of buying and installing a multimedia system.

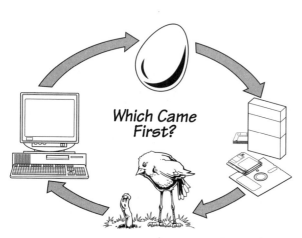

Which Came First?

▶ Which comes first, faster computers or more powerful software? Similar to the age-old "chicken and the egg" scenario, computer and software technology continually drive each other to higher and higher levels and are dependent on each other, blurring the distinction between which comes first.

PART 4

Getting Multimedia to Work

While you may be ready to jump feet first into multimedia this very moment, your computer might not be up to the task quite yet. Unless you purchased your computer system with multimedia in mind, you may find yourself staring down at a machine incapable of providing a decent interactive experience. And nothing is quite as frustrating as having a computer that can almost provide multimedia, except perhaps having a properly equipped machine that is incapable, for some unknown reason, of actually delivering the goods.

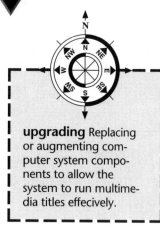

upgrading Replacing or augmenting computer system components to allow the system to run multimedia titles effecively.

Laying the Groundwork

Luckily, there are a few routes to getting the majority of computers purchased within the past few years up and running multimedia in no time. If your computer is almost capable of providing multimedia, there may be the option of *upgrading* those components that are holding the system hostage. Here, you must identify which pieces are the weak links in the multimedia chain, and replace or augment them with multimedia-capable components. Refer to Appendix A to find out if your current system is multimedia capable, or simply read on if you already know your system needs to be upgraded.

If your system is already multimedia capable, but you are unable to use multimedia titles on the machine, you will need to do a little techno-sleuthing. If your current computer works fine with all but a few multimedia products, chances are there is an improperly installed or configured component crippling the system, which prevents you from using some titles on an otherwise perfectly adequate machine. Here you'll need to spend some time finding out where the problem actually is, and either fix it yourself or, better still, have a qualified technician fix it for you.

Whether you are looking to upgrade your existing computer in order to deliver cost-effective multimedia or must find and remedy a problem with an existing multimedia-capable machine, you'll find the assistance and advice of a professional technician invaluable. While these technology specialists were once difficult to locate and expensive to procure the services of, today you'll be pleasantly surprised to find them at nearly every twist and turn in the multimedia maze, ready to avail their services at a price you are more likely to find reasonable.

While you'll usually have no problem keeping your multimedia machine in good working order once it has been properly set up and configured, getting it up and running can prove more of a challenge than you might expect. And since your time and sanity are generally worth more than the cost of a qualified technician, I'd strongly suggest befriending one of these folks before going too much further. However, the technically astute and adventurous will probably skip this section altogether, and so the remainder of this part of the book is really for those of us who don't relish the idea of spending a weekend or two up to our hips in upgrade cards, cables, and heavily caffeinated beverages.

► *After a day of techno-sleuthing, a session of multimedia sleuthing can help calm your nerves. (from Creative Multimedia's* Who Killed Sam Rupert?)

Finding a Qualified Technician

Locating a good computer technician is a lot like finding a good car mechanic. It may take a little effort on your part, but once you've formed a solid relationship with one, you'll find your mind a little more at ease and your nights a bit more restful. A good technician you can trust will take much of the worry out of owning a multimedia computer, just as a good mechanic takes the worry out of owning an automobile. But where can you find a qualified technician to take the difficulty out of multimedia without taking you for a ride at the same time?

Vendor Provided Support

It all depends on where you are, not only in terms of geographic locations, but in also in terms of your computer setup. If you have already purchased a multimedia computer, or have recently purchased a system you are considering upgrading to multimedia status, you should start by contacting the vendor of your system. Chances are your computer vendor has technicians on staff who are trained to help customers such as yourself get the most from their investment. Since buying a computer isn't a trivial matter, most responsible and business-savvy vendors supply a free period of technical support to ensure their customers remain satisfied with their purchase. Unhappy customers aren't likely to recommend their vendor to friends and family, and many vendors rely on word of mouth to grow their business in the competitive computer industry.

User Group Technicians

If you have not already invested in a computer system or the technical support plan for your existing system has expired, you won't have the luxury of dialing a toll-free number to reach a qualified technician. In this case, you'll have to do a little more legwork to find the technician best suited for your needs. Your first stop should be your local user group.

User groups not only provide a wealth of information and resources for existing computer users, they can be incredibly valuable for those who have not yet made the plunge. Many user groups provide training and consulting services for members who are looking to get the best bang for their buck when it comes to purchasing new multimedia computers or upgrading an existing system. If these services aren't provided by a user group, chances are they can put you in touch with a reputable technician with whom the group has already established a relationship.

A membership to a good computer user group is one of the most valuable investments a computer owner can make, and can be just as valuable to those who need advice on a new purchase or upgrade — you don't have to already own a computer in order to get your money's worth from a user group. For more information on finding a good user group, see Part 6.

Superstore Technicians

If you are unable to find a qualified technician through your computer vendor or user group, you may consider looking at your nearest computer "superstore" for assistance. CompUSA, MicroCenter, Egghead Software, and other national computer software and hardware stores not only sell computer goods, but many provide excellent technical support services as well.

Walk into your nearest computer superstore and ask any sales person what type of in-house technical support they offer. Explain that you are looking for a technician with experience in multimedia systems and upgrades (if that's the case), and would need assistance provided by phone or in person. Since technical support has become an important competitive factor for all computer vendors, whether they sell direct or through computer superstores, chances are you'll find a qualified technician capable of helping you set up your multimedia system, upgrade your existing system, or track down and resolve any problems that may appear along the way.

▶ It doesn't take a math wizard to calculate the savings gained by hiring a properly trained technician to help install your multimedia system. (from Brøderbund's Math Workshop)

Computer Consultants

If you are unable to find a superstore technician, and had no luck with your computer vendor or user group, you might have to enlist the services of a professional consulting agency. To find these folks, simply look in the classified advertisements of your local newspaper or yellow pages directory under "Computer Consulting." While generally more expensive than the other methods listed here, professional computer consultants often perform support services others will not, such as house calls. Rather than packing up your computer and taking it into a superstore for help, or spending hours on the phone with technical support, one big advantage to professional consultants is their flexibility when it comes to service. Simply pick a time that is best for the consultant to visit your home or office, and have a fresh pot of coffee brewing when they arrive.

Technicians in Training

If none of these methods of finding a good technician is possible, or none appeal to you, you might find the perfect match for your needs and budget at your local college or, in some cases, even high school. Believe it or not, many of the best people in the business aren't actually in the business at all. They are, in fact, in the classroom.

To find these technical support diamonds in the rough, begin by calling your local college's main number and asking to speak with the director of the computer science department. I would recommend going through the colleges in your area first, and as a last resort turning to the high schools.

In either case, once you get through to the appropriate person, explain that you are looking for a responsible computer science student who has experience with the type of computer you own. Ask if they can recommend a student willing to work on your particular project, be it setting up a multimedia system or upgrading your existing computer. Make it clear that you want a student with experience and references of prior work. You'll also need to find someone who can fit your work into his or her school schedule. Although you may have to sacrifice a good degree of professionalism when employing the services of a student, the advantages can make it worthwhile.

Students are quite flexible in their evening and weekend hours since they go to school during weekdays, and so may fit into your schedule much better than a professional. Their services also cost a fraction of what you'll pay for the professional technician, and students often bring unbridled enthusiasm and dedication to a project. However, just as with professionals, it's a good idea to have fresh coffee on hand when they arrive. (In the case of high school students who haven't yet found the joys of java, a cold soda will usually do the trick.)

There is the risk, however, that a student will get midway through your project and then lose interest before completing the work. To avoid this potential disaster, agree to pay the student only after a specified amount of work has been completed. Also, attempt to set up a work schedule with the student to ensure your project is getting consistent attention until it is completed. While professionals bring with them the skills and responsibility needed to juggle various projects and ensure that each is completed more or less on time, the student is usually preoccupied with more interesting things than your computer system and so is most productive when working according to a schedule established before the project even begins.

Is a Technician Really Necessary?

While many people have no problem setting up their own multimedia computer (or upgrade an existing system without a hitch), at some point nearly everyone finds themselves staring bleary-eyed and angrily at their computer while doing everything within their power to keep from hurtling a bowling ball through the monitor of the once-cherished possession.

This, of course, assumes you haven't already ripped your hair out trying to make sense of the hundreds of options and features available when it comes to multimedia computers and upgrades. Sure, this book gives you a good starting point for getting the most from multimedia, but this is an industry infamous for rapidly evolving technology and overnight obsolescence of state-of-the-art equipment. While some people truly enjoy keeping up with the changes and challenges of computer technology, just as many of us simply want to enjoy our computers with as little effort and interruption as possible.

I've seen countless friends and family members plunk down a substantial chunk of cash or credit for computer equipment that ultimately sits unused in the corner of their basement or attic because they either made a bad purchase to begin with or were unable to get the system to work properly once they got it home. With only a few hours of help from a properly trained technician, however, they would have been well on their way to a fabulous multimedia experience rather than watching their investment slowly waste away in the corner of the room.

Setting Up a New Multimedia Machine

If you decide to forego a technician and brave the multimedia computer world without assistance, you're most likely to find setting up a new multimedia computer the easiest path to follow. When you are dealing with a new multimedia computer, all of the instructions detailing how to assemble the system come with the computer and each of the components are preselected to work seamlessly with each other.

As multimedia computers become more and more consumer oriented, their complexity in terms of setup becomes more and more manageable. People simply want to take their new computer home, plug in a few cables, and be up and running with a minimum of effort. Understanding this, most computer vendors attempt to make it as easy as possible to use their systems. Many of today's new multimedia computers come preinstalled; all of the software and specialized hardware is installed at the factory, meaning you need only plug the monitor, keyboard, and mouse into the computer, and the computer itself into a power outlet. In this case the sound card, video card, and even CD-ROM drive are already installed, together with the operating system and whatever software may have come with the computer. With preinstalled multimedia computers, you'll be up and running in less time than it takes to close this book, grab a quick snack, and hunker down in front of your new system.

To further ease the burden of setting up a new multimedia system, some systems even include a video tape of how to go about installing and using your new investment. The Compaq Presario I received on an evaluation basis while writing this book not only came with everything preinstalled, it also came with an easy-to-understand video tape to help me get the system up and running as fast as possible. The arrival of sophisticated computers that are easy to install and use is one of the great benefits of today's consumer-oriented multimedia revolution. People simply don't want to spend all weekend (or longer) struggling to get their new computers working properly, and many vendors have responded to this demand.

But what if you happen to buy a multimedia computer that doesn't come preinstalled? Instead, your system may have come in the form of a bunch of individual boxes, with everything from the video card to the operating system needing to be manually installed. What then? Well, the first thing you'll want to do is find a large block of time in your schedule to dedicate to the installation process. I would set aside at least three hours of uninterrupted time, understanding beforehand that this may not be enough if a problem surfaces during installation. Next, you'll need to locate the user guide for your new computer. The user guide, or owner's manual, is typically found in the same box as the computer itself. While each piece of computer equipment generally comes with an owner's manual describing that particular piece of equipment in detail, you must first find the user guide, which gives an overview of your new computer system as a whole and explains step by step how to assemble the entire package.

Reading the Manual

Most computer systems come with a thin manual that says, "Read Me First" or something similar, on the cover. This is one document you don't want to lose or ignore. The "Read Me First" booklet will tell you what things to look out for when installing your new machine, and often includes valuable advice that can save you a good deal of time during the installation process. Before you begin assembling your new computer, be sure to search each box for a "Read Me First" manual or notice. Failure to read each "Read Me First" document might not only result in a lot of unnecessary frustration and lost time, but in some cases can lead to serious system damage when assembling the various pieces of your new computer.

Registering Your New Computer

While you are looking for the "Read Me First" document, keep your eyes peeled for a product registration card. Often times each piece of equipment comes with its own registration card. Don't toss these out! Instead, put them aside to fill out later. If you don't register your new computer, there is a very good chance you won't receive technical support or important notices from your computer vendor. Since technical support is usually supplied free of charge for a period of time after purchasing your new system, you may be asked to include a photocopy of your purchase receipt.

When you have located the "Read Me First" booklet and begin to read it for valuable time-saving tips and directions, be on the look-out for technical support information. Technical support is often crucial when installing a new machine, and so you'll want to have the telephone number for the vendor's technical support service written down where you'll be sure to find it if you run into a problem. Many technical support services require a special code or serial number when you call to verify that you are indeed the owner of the new machine. Be sure to note any special numbers or codes required for technical support, and write them down as well. Having all of your technical support information in a single, easily accessible location will make the installation process go much smoother if you need to call for help.

Beginning the Installation

The basics of installing most multimedia systems are, by and large, the same. First, you attach the power cables to the computer and video monitor, and then plug them into a nearby power outlet. With the power for every system component turned off, remove the computer cover and install the video and sound cards into the system. If the CD-ROM drive is an internal unit that didn't come preinstalled, it also should be installed before closing up the system. After the cards are installed and the cover is on, you'll plug the external speakers into the sound card and the video monitor into the video card. If the CD-ROM drive is an external unit, it is then plugged into the appropriate *interface adapter board* (usually part of the sound card). Finally, the keyboard and mouse are connected to the computer. Voilà — the system is assembled!

interface adapter board A board, or card, located inside the computer that is used to connect external devices such as the monitor, CD-ROM drive, and speakers.

Although these steps are basically the same no matter which computer system you are assembling, each vendor provides step-by-step instructions describing exactly how the steps are to be carried out. Generally these instructions are found in the "Read Me First" manual. At the very least, this document describes where to find the step-by-step instructions. In addition to these detailed instructions, vendors supply clearly labeled diagrams that illustrate how and where the cards and cables are to be attached.

It's a good idea to review the installation steps and diagrams beforehand, ensuring you not only have the proper tools for the job but also have the appropriate instructions for your computer components. Although it is rare, occasionally the wrong instructions

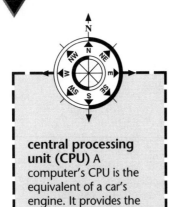

central processing unit (CPU) A computer's CPU is the equivalent of a car's engine. It provides the raw power on which all other parts rely. Although there are many facets to a computer, the CPU is usually considered the heart of any system.

ship with a computer, or a piece of equipment or connector cable may be missing. To save time and wasted effort during the installation process, be sure to review your setup and the various steps involved before beginning the installation.

Although most multimedia computers can be assembled by the new owner, some vendors require that specific upgrades and components be installed only by an authorized technician. In this case, performing the work yourself may void any warranty provided with your computer. Here, the components are generally those you wouldn't want to mess around with yourself anyway, such as CPU upgrades, and are best left to technicians who have the proper tools and who are properly trained to perform the work.

Upgrading Your Current Machine to Multimedia

If you already own a computer, but it isn't multimedia capable, it may be possible to upgrade the various pieces of your system as needed, thereby obtaining perfectly adequate multimedia without the cost of purchasing a new computer altogether. For details on deciding whether to upgrade your current system or simply to invest in a new multimedia system altogether, refer to Appendix A. If you have already decided that upgrading is the right choice for you, you'll have to decide on how to go about upgrading your system.

Buying an Upgrade Kit

While it is possible to individually buy each piece of equipment required for your multimedia upgrade, it is often easier and cheaper to simply purchase an *upgrade kit*. Upgrade kits come in a variety of configurations and price ranges, but they generally include the same pieces of equipment: a sound card, audio speakers, and a CD-ROM drive. These three components form the basis of almost every multimedia upgrade kit, but many also include a few multimedia titles to get you started. The quality of each upgrade kit varies, as do the individual components that comprise each kit. Also, don't expect each component of a multimedia upgrade kit to be created by the same vendor. Most upgrade kits are simply a bundle of hardware components and software products created by a variety of vendors.

upgrade kit Multimedia hardware bundles that feature the necessary equipment to make an existing computer system multimedia capable. These upgrade kits typically include a sound card and speakers, CD-ROM drive, and a number of multimedia titles.

The price of upgrade kits varies almost as much as the quality of kits themselves. It is possible to find kits priced under $300, while many are over $600. The difference in price is generally, but not always, a reflection of the quality of each item in the kit. As a rule of thumb, the more expensive the kit is, the better the quality of its components. However, it's also possible for an expensive kit to have a pretty lousy collection of components. Like nearly everything else you buy, it's a good idea to keep your eyes open and compare the various kits available before you make a decision to invest in one. To ensure that you purchase the best upgrade kit for your particular system, locate and read current industry magazine and journal reviews of the upgrade kits you are considering.

It's also a good idea to understand the various pieces of equipment that make up a multimedia upgrade kit, further ensuring that you get the best deal possible when comparison shopping. Since you now know the basics of each component in a multimedia computer, you already know the basics of each component in an upgrade kit. However, it's worth taking a closer look at each of these components to get a better idea of what to look for when evaluating upgrade kits.

CD-ROM drive A device that makes it possible for your computer to use CD-ROMs, a variation of the audio CD. A single CD-ROM holds the equivalent of nearly 600 low capacity floppy disks and typically contain graphics, sound, and/or text. The CD-ROM drive gives your computer access to the information found on CD-ROMs.

CD-ROM drive

The industry standard CD-ROM drive *speed* is 2x, or double-speed. It's fine to invest in a faster speed drive, such as the 3x (triple-speed) or 4x (quadruple-speed), but never consider a 1x (single-speed) drive. Chances are you won't even find an upgrade kit on the market that includes these older CD-ROM drives, but you might run across a single-speed drive (or kit containing a single-speed drive) in the clearance area of a computer superstore or during an inventory reduction sale.

Stay as far away from the single-speed CD-ROM drives as possible, since you'll never get satisfactory performance from these units when running today's multimedia titles. Double-speed drives, on the other hand, are a good investment and are plentiful and relatively inexpensive these days. Faster CD-ROM drives really aren't a necessity, since most titles available on the market today don't take advantage of their added speed. You can rest easy knowing a double-speed drive will play the majority of multimedia titles now available with fine performance.

CD-ROM drives require an interface adapter board installed on the computer into which you'll plug the drive's data cables. Apple Macintosh computers come with this board already installed, which is known as a *SCSI interface* (Small Computer System Interface, pronounced "scuzzy," which is widely used in the Macintosh world). Windows-based computers, on the other hand, do not typically have the interface adapter board preinstalled and so you'll have to buy and install one. Several of the multimedia upgrade kits now available for Windows-based computers include the CD-ROM drive interface adapter board, however, making upgrading a bit easier. The CD-ROM unit can often be connected directly to the sound card, meaning you don't have to install a separate adapter board to get your drive up and running.

In the Windows world, it is important to ensure that the CD-ROM drive you buy is compatible with the sound card you'll be installing. Luckily, multimedia upgrade kits match these components for you. If you are buying each piece individually, however, you need to be sure each part of the upgrade is compatible with the others. While the same is true for Macintosh upgrades, conflicts are more common when assembling a variety of Windows components. Therefore, Windows users should take extra care to ensure that multimedia components are compatible with each other (and the overall computer system) before they are purchased.

Sound card

The Macintosh line of computers comes with a built-in sound card, meaning these computer users need only install a set of speakers to hear the audio portion of multimedia titles. Windows-based computers, however, generally require that a sound card be manually installed, to which the audio speakers are then connected. There are many sound cards on the market today, and so you should know what to look for when evaluating upgrade kits:

speed The speed of a CD-ROM drive is a measure of how fast it can get information from the surface of a CD-ROM to you, also known as the *data transfer rate.* Currently there are four different speeds to choose from when evaluating CD-ROM drives: single (1x), double (2x), triple (3x), and quadruple (4x).

SCSI interface The interface adapter board that comes preinstalled on Apple Macintosh computers, also available as an option on Windows-based systems.

synthesizer The part of a sound card that creates music and sound effects.

▶ *Synthesizer* — This is the part of a sound card that creates music and sound effects. There are two different types of synthesizers to choose from: FM (Frequency Modulation) and wave-table. *Wave-table synthesizers* play digital recordings of sounds, producing the better quality audio of the two. Because of their higher quality sound production, the multimedia market is shifting towards wave-table synthesizers. In order to get the best investment for your dollar, choose a sound card that uses a wave-table synthesizer.

wave-table synthe-sizers Synthesizers that play digital recordings of sounds, producing better quality audio than FM synthesizers. Because of their higher quality sound produc-tion, the multimedia market is shifting towards wave-table synthesizers.

synthesizer voices The different voices a synthesizer can produce. An important measure of a synthesizer's quality is the number of voices it can produce.

digitized Something that has been converted to computer format, such as artwork or sound.

MIDI (Musical Instrument Digital Interface) Specialized music technology that provides the ability to record and/or play back musical instruments using the computer.

▶ *Synthesizer Voices* — An important measure of a synthesizer's quality is the number of voices it can produce. While 32 synthesizer voices is standard for very high quality sound cards, good sound can be produced with fewer voices. For most purposes, 20 or more synthesizer voices is considered adequate for good sound, and so you should consider only those sound cards that have 20 voices or more.

▶ *Digital Audio Playback and Recording* — Not only are today's sound cards capable of synthesizing music and sound effects, they are also capable of playing and recording digital audio. Digital audio played on sound cards is the same as that found on digital audio CDs, and is a different source of audio than what is created by a syn-thesizer. Since they are two different types of sound, synthesized sound and digital audio can be played at the same time. For instance, a digital audio music sound track can thump along while your spaceship in a video game blasts away with realistic sound effects created by the synthesizer. Since sound card digital audio is the same as that found on audio CDs, you should expect your sound card to both record and play back with the same fidelity: 16-bit, 44.1kHz stereo sound.

▶ *Line In/Line Out* — In order to connect devices to your sound card, a *line in connector* must be present. Using line in you can connect a num-ber of audio devices, such as an audio CD player, your home stereo, or even the audio portion of a video cassette player. Essentially, a line in connector allows you to bring audio into the computer. *A line out connector,* on the other hand, allows you to play computer sounds on devices located outside your computer. Using line out you can connect a set of headphones, speakers, or any other device to your computer that would allow you to hear sound.

▶ *Other Standard Features* — You'll find a few other standard features on today's audio cards, including a *game port,* which allows you to connect a joystick or other video game controller to your computer, and a *microphone input port,* which allows you to record sound from your own digital audio sources directly into your computer. These features are common to all modern sound cards, and so you can be sure that any card worth buying will include both a game port and microphone input port.

Audio speakers

While you may initially think that any set of audio speakers is good enough for multimedia, true multimedia speakers are actually specifically designed for computer use. Using nonmultimedia speakers might, in fact, damage your computer! Two features distinguish multimedia speakers from standard audio speakers: *magnetic shielding* and the ability to run on their own power.

Magnetic shielding means the magnets inside the speakers have been properly covered with special materials to ensure they do no damage to computer devices. Standard audio speakers are not shielded, and if placed close to computer equipment can cause significant damage resulting from the magnetic field. While it's possible to place unshielded speakers far

line in connector Sound card feature that allows you to connect to the card a number of devices, such as an audio CD player, your home stereo, or even the audio portion of a video cassette player.

line out connector Sound card feature that allows you to play computer sounds on devices located outside your computer.

game port Standard feature on an audio card, allowing you to connect a joystick or other video game controller to your computer.

microphone input port Standard feature on an audio card, allowing you to record sound from your own digital audio sources directly into your computer.

magnetic shielding
Proper covering of the magnets inside the speakers to ensure they do no damage to computer devices.

enough away from the computer so as to pose no serious threat, it's best to invest in a pair of shielded speakers specifically designed for multimedia use.

The ability for speakers to run on their own power, either using batteries or a power cable, is nearly as important as magnetic shielding. If speakers are not self-powered, your multimedia audio might sound weak or be impossible to hear at all. While your home stereo has enough power to pump sound through standard speakers, the computer simply doesn't have sufficient amplifier wattage to produce good sound through standard speakers. Using self-powered speakers, however, resolves this problem altogether.

Goodies

Many upgrade kits come bundled with quality product titles, allowing you to jump into multimedia action as soon as the upgrade is completed. Usually a reference product, such as a multimedia encyclopedia, is included, together with a few entertainment titles. The retail price of these goodies alone often exceeds what you'll end up paying for the upgrade kit itself, with the quality and number of titles helping you deciding between upgrade kits that are very close in terms of components and price.

Some of the products included with multimedia upgrade kits are the full versions of commercially available titles, while others are simply demonstration versions or are limited editions of a commercial product. There is a big difference between a *demo version*, a *limited edition*, and the *full version*. Some demos are nothing more than a slick graphical presentation, which gives you a rough idea of what the actual product is like. With these demonstrations you can't interact with the product at all, and can only watch as the advertisement parades across your screen. Other demos are usable, however, and allow you to test drive the commercial product in a very limited way. These demos are often called limited edition products, so named because some features and content are missing, which the vendor hopes will inspire you to purchase the full commercial version.

Don't be misled by multimedia kits that have only demos and limited edition software as goodies. Many upgrade kits give you the real thing, fully functional commercial products ready to be used as soon as the upgrade is complete. These are the goodies to keep your eyes peeled for, since demos and limited edition products aren't worth bothering with when you can usually get the full versions of the same products if you look hard enough.

Putting It All Together

Once you have purchased a multimedia upgrade kit, you'll have to install the various components in order to get up and running. Every upgrade kit comes with installation instructions, and it is important to follow them to the letter. Just as with new multimedia computers, upgrade kits often include a "Read Me First" booklet, which gives step-by-step installation instructions. And, just as with multimedia computers, failure to follow these instructions can result in permanent damage to your system.

Macintosh users have it easy. Since sound cards and adapter boards come built-in with most Macintoshes, these computer users need only plug in the speakers and CD-ROM drive and they are up and running with their new multimedia system. Windows users, however, must install

demo version A demonstration version of a software product. Demo versions are often nothing more than multimedia presentations that give you a rough idea of a particular product, although sometimes a demo is a product that can be used in a very limited capacity (see limited edition).

limited edition A scaled-down version of a software product, often lacking in features or content in order to persuade the customer to purchase the full version.

full version The complete, commercially available version of a software product. The full version of a product is not limited in any way, and is what you would expect if you were to purchase the product at the full price.

the sound card and CD-ROM interface adapter board (if not part of the sound card) themselves. This can be a little intimidating, since it means opening up the computer and fooling around with the sensitive guts of your system.

To make matters worse, it's possible to kill your computer entirely if you don't install the sound card and CD-ROM interfacer adapter board properly. This is where I strongly recommend a qualified technician who has performed similar upgrade operations before. The stress and worry of putting your computer six feet under by mistake isn't worth it. Hire a professional if you can, and save yourself a boat load of anxiety (and money, in the event your computer unexpectedly kicks the bucket during a do-it-yourself upgrade).

I recommend purchasing your upgrade kit from a computer superstore if at all possible, for a number of reasons:

1. You'll know what you are getting before you pay for it. Chances are the best upgrade kit deals are installed on a computer and are on display at the superstore, so you'll be able to shop and compare based on actual performance rather than by comparing product specifications.

2. You'll have a chance to speak at length with a knowledge-able sales person.

3. You can often have your upgrade kit installed for a very reasonable fee the day you buy it.

If you decide to perform the multimedia upgrade yourself, here are a few guidelines for you:

1. Follow the instructions provided in the kit.

2. Turn off *all* components of your computer before you start the upgrade. While turning your computer off may appear to also turn off the monitor, the monitor may simply have

gone blank because no video signal is available once the computer is turned off. Be sure the power switch for your monitor and all other devices attached to your computer are in the off position before you begin the upgrade.

▶ 3. Wear static free clothing, such as cotton, and avoid highly static materials when performing the upgrade.

When the upgrade is complete, you'll surely be anxious to flip the power switch on your new pride and joy, and drink in the wonders of your new system. Go for it! But don't be surprised if your initial excitement quickly turns to a deep sense of despair. It's not unusual to turn on your new multimedia computer only to find none of your multimedia software titles work properly, or worse yet the machine freezes up entirely. The heartache and disappointment can be profound when this happens, and will quickly be replaced by utter frustration if not anger.

Before you blow your top, however, it might help to know that most of the problems you'll encounter are easily remedied with a solid dose of patience, the user guide, and a technical support call or two. Take a deep breath, a quick stroll around the yard, and jump back into formation. Multimedia commandos don't admit defeat so easily, and if you've come this far you are practically on the threshold of success. Don't give up.

When Getting Multimedia to Work Doesn't Quite Work

Although it is very frustrating to rush home and install your new multimedia computer or upgrade kit only to find things don't work as expected when you are finally done, this is the reality of today's computer systems. In the future computers will be as foolproof as our televisions, microwave ovens, and toasters. Until then, however, we must gird ourselves with a positive attitude towards trouble-shooting and problem solving. Think of it not as an inconvenience, but as an adventure!

OK, it really is an inconvenience and a terribly annoying one at that. You expect this thing to work like a charm and instead you'll have to perform what amounts to black magic just to get it up and running. Troubleshooting to solve computer problems isn't everyone's cup of tea, yet at one point or another you'll likely run into a situation that requires some degree of technology sleuthing.

Calling Technical Support

The fastest way to resolve a problem is by using your telephone to dial the technical support department of your multimedia computer (or upgrade kit) vendor. Newly purchased equipment is covered under warranty, and so you shouldn't hesitate to call upon technical support to help solve your problem. Have any serial number or special codes required for access to technical support handy when you call. Also, have the name and model number of the product you are having problems with at hand. You'll speed the process up considerably by providing the support technicians with this information at the beginning of your call.

While technical support is your best bet for solving problems with your new equipment, you might find yourself in need of help at a time when support isn't available. Not all technical support departments are open over the weekend or in the late evening. Since many people find these hours most convenient to install new equipment, they often find themselves in need of help when none is available. If you can afford to wait until the technical support department is available, do so. If not, you'll find yourself hip deep in computer jargon and cryptic computer commands in an attempt to solve the problem.

Figuring It Out on Your Own

Begin by looking inside your computer user manual (or upgrade kit manual) for a section entitled "Troubleshooting," "Problems," "Errors," or something similar. This part of the manual typically gives a listing of the most common problems you'll encounter, together with their solutions. Every component in a computer is unique, and far too many variations exist to even begin suggesting what problems you might encounter. Your best bet is to first contact technical support and consult your installation manual if needed.

Buying Smart

The only foolproof method of getting your multimedia computer or upgrade kit to work is to purchase your equipment only from reputable vendors, with a money-back guarantee and at least 30 days of free technical support. Anything less, and you may find yourself clearing a corner of your basement or attic to make room for the equipment you had such high hopes for.

Following these guidelines, however, not only gives you the ability to work closely with qualified technical support during the installation process, but also gives you the right to return products as necessary for exchange with a multimedia computer or upgrade kit that works as promised. While as many as 30 percent of all upgrade kits purchased are returned for one reason or another, buying fully warranted products from respected vendors, reading the installation guidelines thoroughly before doing a stitch of work, and having the telephone number of a qualified technical support person can help to ensure that you are one of the 70 percent who find the process of getting multimedia to work extremely rewarding.

Who Is Creating Multimedia?

Being surrounded by multimedia, in its many forms, it is often easy to forget that there are real people behind the scenes making it all work. Of course, without computers, multimedia as we know it today wouldn't be possible. But without the many creative minds behind those computers, there really wouldn't be many multimedia products worth getting excited about.

▶ *Hollywood has embraced multimedia, with nearly every film produced today taking advantage of this exciting technology. From* The Terminator *to* Jurassic Park *to* Forrest Gump, *multimedia technology is used to produce both subtle and spectacular special effects that captivate and thrill audiences of all ages.*

Multimedia Hollywood

The next two parts of this book focus on the multimedia industry as a profession, a place you might enjoy working. The best way to introduce any profession is through introducing the players, the "who's who" in the industry. And if there's any place worth looking at, a place that prides itself on good looks and a killer image, a yin to the glitz and sex appeal of multimedia's yang, it would have to be Hollywood.

I first realized how the promise of technology would eventually change the face of our world some 15 years ago, at about the time I waded into the computer industry myself. It wasn't some profound-thinking technology guru who led me to enlightenment, or serendipity working in my favor, or anything even close to deep and meaningful. Quite the opposite actually. I have Hollywood to thank.

Synthetic Actors in a Real World

I was watching a made-for-TV movie that I can barely remember today. In fact, the only thing I can recall about this movie is one single scene. In this movie, a group of rogue film producers had assembled a truckload of computer equipment that could generate incredibly realistic synthetic actors.

These computer-generated actors looked and acted exactly like their human counterparts, yet were a heck of a lot easier to deal with and didn't demand a paycheck let alone the usual ego massage. And since these synthetic actors lived only in the computer, they could be programmed to do anything the script demanded. Wham-o. No more wasted film, time, or talent. It was all in the computer.

However, there was a catch: in order to generate a synthetic actor, a human actor was first needed to feed the various facial expressions and voice intonations into the computer. The evil filmmakers would convince naive actors to sign away all rights to the use of their likenesses while putting them through a variety of poses and readings that would later be fed into the computer, ultimately making these poor humans obsolete.

▶ *Live actors are often used as models for the characters in multimedia action titles.* (from Origin's BioForge)

The details of the movie aren't important today, and weren't very important even back then. The only scene I now recall involved a gaggle of actors and actresses playing a spirited game of volleyball on the beach while a van loaded with computer equipment manned by unscrupulous film executives recorded the festivities. At that moment I realized computer technology capable of creating lifelike simulations would someday make the transition from made-for-TV drama to real-life drama. And that time is now upon us, believe it or not.

Completely realistic synthetic actors won't spring up overnight, however. Although under constant development, this technology is still years away. In the meantime, Hollywood has finally grasped the power of multimedia and you can bet it will wring out every last drop of it during its quest for the ultimate entertainment experience. You know and recognize multimedia used in television commercials, which is now passé. The bigger and better deal is being born in the studios of Hollywood, in particular at DreamWorks SDK.

DreamWorks SDK
A Hollywood studio founded by entertainment industry gurus Steven Spielberg, Jeffrey Katzenberg, and David Geffen. Expect DreamWorks SDK to explode on the multimedia scene, arriving in every vehicle capable of delivering its products to the masses: Movie theaters, televisions, home entertainment systems, and home computers are among the vehicles targeted.

DreamWorks SDK

If you've been blown away by multimedia special effects dazzling theatergoers over the past few years, hang on tightly to your seat. Dinosaurs living and playing in harmony with people on remote islands in the tropics is child's play compared to what Steven Spielberg, Jeffrey Katzenberg, and David Geffen are dreaming up.

The trio have formed their own Hollywood studio, DreamWorks SDK. Banking heavily on the power of multimedia combined with the power of their own creative genius plus a little help and financial investment from friends Bill Gates of Microsoft and Paul Allen (formerly of Microsoft and now owner of the interactive company Starwave), DreamWorks SDK will usher in a new world of entertainment when their first film hits the screen sometime in late 1996.

What the trio will bring to bear on the entertainment industry is nothing less than a stupendous mix of power in every major area of multimedia. Spielberg will handle the film end of the business, while Geffen (whose music company Geffen Records is a powerhouse in its own right) will handle the music side of things, with Katzenberg rounding out the crew with his expertise in animation, honed while a top executive at Disney. Toss in all the interactive multimedia muscle Gates' Microsoft and Allen's Starwave have to flex, plus a dash of old-fashioned good luck, and you're looking at the nucleus of an organization destined to supply much of the world's best entertainment for the first few decades of the coming millennium, if not longer.

DreamWorks SDK is not only coming to a theater near you, but also to your television and multimedia computer. These folks aren't missing a beat, and aim to bring their entertainment to you in any form they can. Expect DreamWorks SDK to explode on the multimedia scene, arriving in every vehicle capable of delivering its products to the masses. Movie theaters, televisions, home entertainment systems, and home computers are among the vehicles targeted by the folks who independently brought you *E.T.*, Madonna, and *The Lion King*. And this time, they are coming down the pike together.

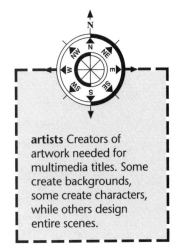

artists Creators of artwork needed for multimedia titles. Some create backgrounds, some create characters, while others design entire scenes.

The Many Faces of Multimedia

It doesn't necessarily take a few million dollars, a roomful of technology gurus, and a background in the film industry to produce compelling multimedia products, although it is a surefire way to get the ball rolling. Yet in most cases, the skills and resources required to assemble a good multimedia product are simply beyond the scope of any single individual. Because of its very nature, multimedia is a complex and multifaceted gem that seems to have a side for nearly everyone.

Since multimedia is essentially the combination of sight and sound with computer technology, there are many areas where people find their niche in this budding industry. Following are just a few of the folks you will find hard at work in the multimedia world.

Artists

When it comes to creating multimedia products, *artists* are found at nearly every twist and turn of the process. Every multimedia product on the market requires some amount of artistic effort, whether it be in the traditional form of oil and paintbrush on canvas, which is later converted to computer form, or true digital artwork created entirely on the computer.

Multimedia software companies often draw on the talent of a wide range of artists, from photographers to pen and ink traditionalists, to cutting-edge computer animators. Some have a great degree of experience in the computer arts, while others have never touched a computer in their lives. Still others provide the invaluable skill of converting traditional artwork into the computer format.

Although these artwork conversion specialists don't create the original artwork, they are considered artists without question, since they must straddle the worlds of traditional and computerized art and be able to convert artwork from one format to the other while maintaining the integrity of the original work. This is hardly something most people would have thought of as a full-blown career. But it is, and a respected one at that.

▶ *Many of the large, rectangular buttons on Mantis Development Corporation's World Wide Web site began as traditional artwork, before being converted to computer format by an artwork conversion specialist.*

Reinventing Art

Multimedia artists break the mold of traditional artists, in the past drawing criticism from many members of the established art world. Only a few years ago, computer artists weren't considered capable of producing true artwork simply because their work was created with a tool not normally employed by artists. For thousands of years the paintbrush and canvas have been the tools of choice for artists around the world. Photography eventually came along, and was initially looked upon as an impure way of creating an image. But time and the work of masters, such as Ansel Adams, ultimately proved that the camera was a very capable tool when in the right hands, and now the computer is emerging from the center of that same debate.

Early detractors claimed the computer made it much too easy for anyone to create what might at first glance look like artwork, but was in fact was merely an impressive collage of images and color requiring no true artistic talent. And while this was a valid argument, at the time very few artists were actually using the computer to create artwork. Computer artwork sprung initially from the fingertips of computer scientists and hackers who were not trained in the arts but were nonetheless creating works of substance capable of sparking the initial debates surrounding computer artwork.

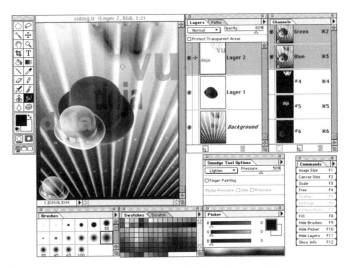

▶ *Adobe Photoshop, one of the most powerful image editing tools on the market today, is used by artists around the world to create original artwork, edit existing artwork, and convert artwork from traditional format to computer format.*

Closing the Debate

Within the past few years, however, the creativity, skill, and vision of true artists splashed upon the computer canvas, answering the question of the computer's place in the art world once and for all. As traditional artists flock to the computer, making it their tool of choice for artistic expression, this debate is being soundly closed. The computer is the most powerful tool for creating artwork ever devised, allowing artists to express themselves as never before with unparalleled ease. The barriers between art and expression are rapidly crumbling, as people who have never been formally trained in the arts find they too are capable of expressing what they see in their mind's eye.

sound engineers
People involved with sound in multimedia apply skills found in the traditional sound industry (such as recording and editing, dubbing, or generating audio effects, to name a few) to the highly technical field of computerized sound.

Sound People

While the visual side to multimedia is for many the most compelling aspect of any given product, the people behind the scenes and at the sound controls are creating magic in their own right. And, just like every other piece of the multimedia pie, there's enough here to go around for everyone.

Sound tracks are the most obvious use of sound in multimedia, although there is more to this aspect of the technology than meets the ear. It isn't enough to have musical talent and to write and record sound tracks. There must also be technically savvy *sound engineers,* who are able to convert the result into computer form. Just as there are artists in the industry whose job entails converting traditional artwork into the computer format, there are audio people who do the same for sound. And they are revered every bit as much as their visually inclined colleagues.

It takes a great deal of technical expertise and an intimate knowledge of the dynamics of audio media to convert traditional sound into computerized sound. Sure, it's fairly straightforward to record audio directly into the computer, but that's only the beginning of what

▶ One of the most important parts of any multimedia action title is the sound. When you play Origin's Wings of Glory, *you see from behind the controls and hear realistic sound to complete the experience.*

these folks do. Not only must computer sound engineers convert the music into computer form while maintaining the integrity of the original work, but they must work within the constraints of a multimedia project. And there are many constraints when it comes to multimedia.

Sound Constraints

To begin with, *digitized* sound must take up as little space on a CD-ROM as possible. While an audio CD is pure music, a multimedia product must also accommodate images, text, and the computer software to tie it all together. Squeezing this all onto a CD-ROM takes some serious effort, and almost always requires special *compression* techniques that crunch the sound and image information down in size. This compressed information must be re-expanded, or decompressed, lightning fast in order to avoid jerky sound and image playback when the user navigates the product. No trivial matter, to be certain. This is where sound engineers really shine, ensuring all the compression and decompression takes place seamlessly in the background without altering the quality of the original sound or affecting the speed of content navigation.

compression Special techniques required to crunch sound and image information down to fit on a CD-ROM.

decompression Techniques used to re-expand CD-ROM data for playback

Sampling Constraints

Sometimes it's not possible to get a decent performance by decompressing previously compressed audio while a multimedia product is in use. Many times, these techniques slow down the overall performance of a product, or result in images and sounds that are so choppy when played they ruin the experience. When this is the case, a sound engineer can re-sample the original sound content.

sampling The process of recording a digital sound.

sample rate A measure of how much audio information is gathered during the sampling process. The higher the sample rate, the higher the quality of sound when played back.

re-sampling A process in which a sound engineer removes portions of the digital audio information until the sound has been whittled down to a more manageable size.

synchronize Ensuring that audio and video play in time (that is, in sync) with each other; for example, making the lips move in time with the voice.

Sampling is commonly used to describe the process of recording a digital sound. The *sample rate* of a recording measures how much audio information is gathered in the process, a reflection of the resulting audio quality — the higher the sample rate, the better the quality of sound when played back. The problem with recording digital sounds at a high sample rate is the large amount of storage space required. The higher the sample rate of a sound, the more space it will take up on the CD-ROM.

When compression techniques aren't doing the trick, it's time to cut away at the sound information itself. By *re-sampling*, a sound engineer removes portions of the digital audio information until the sound has been whittled down to a more manageable size. Although re-sampling an audio source reduces its storage requirement and makes it easier to play back without slowing down the system, it also reduces the final quality of the sound. Audio content that has been re-sampled too much can sound lousy when played back. A sound engineer must carefully balance the re-sampling process to ensure enough audio information is removed to allow smooth playback without taking so much away that it ruins the quality of sound.

Synchronization Constraints

Another difficulty with multimedia sound products is in the ability to *synchronize* audio and video sources. In fact, some sound engineers dedicate their time and skill to ensuring audio and video play in sync with each other; making the lips move in time with the voice. This may at first seem insignificant, but it is not. In the real world we expect people's lips to correspond to the words they are speaking, except perhaps on New Year's Eve. This is pretty easy for us, since we merely speak and our lips move in synch with our voice. This is not the way things work on the computer.

In the computer world, video and audio are independent of each other. It takes special software and even specially skilled sound engineers to ensure the two synchronize realistically. The same goes for any video and sound played in sync on a computer. For example, when a bomb explodes, we expect to see and hear it at once.

technology wizards
Hardware and software gurus who make it possible to combine audio and visual content with computer interactivity.

These are just a few of the places where people seek fame and fortune in the multimedia sound world, but certainly they aren't the only areas. Just as with the visual side of multimedia productions, creating quality sound requires the combined skills and creative talents of many different people. If you take the complexity of the traditional music industry and then slap the added complexity of the film, art, and computer industries on top, you can begin to see why so many diverse talents are required during the production of a multimedia title.

Technology Wizards

At the heart of every multimedia product sit the *technology wizards,* hardware and software gurus who make it possible to combine audio and visual content with computer interactivity. Fear them, loathe them, love them, but above all else, respect them. For without technology wizards, there would be no multimedia magic to begin with.

▶ *Technology wizards call upon a wide range of software tools to create multimedia magic, bringing content to life as they develop interactive products.*

central processing unit (CPU) A computer's CPU is the equivalent of a car's engine. It provides the raw power on which all other parts rely. Although there are many facets to a computer, the CPU is usually considered the heart of any system.

authoring tools Software programs used to create multimedia products.

Technology wizards come in all shapes and sizes, with expertise in more areas than you can shake a magic wand at. Some train their sights entirely on hardware, molding computer video and audio boards from little more than silicon and electricity, while an elite group of hardware magicians conjures up the soul of every computer system, the *central processing unit (CPU)*.

Then there are those who brew the software products we rely on, from operating systems to multimedia *authoring tools*, without which the computer is just about useless. The world of software developers is extremely large; expertise comes from all corners of the map. Some weave spells of video and audio excellence, while others charm the bits and bytes of interactivity.

Technology wizards, whether hardware or software, are perhaps the largest group of individuals contributing to the creation of multimedia products. Their vast powers, however, will slowly shift to our hands as more and more authoring products are developed that make it possible for the nontechnical, everyday person to create multimedia titles. The learning curve for most multimedia authoring tools is still quite steep, and the

▶ *Authoring tools are the foundation of every multimedia product, including edutainment programs such as MECC's* Yukon Trail.

resources expensive and varied, although new products are being developed every day that can put the magic in our hands. And while eventually there will be more multimedia authoring wizards in this world than pure technology wizards, there will remain a highly esteemed group of hardware and software developers who make it possible for the masses to cast their very own multimedia spells.

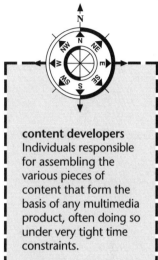

content developers
Individuals responsible for assembling the various pieces of content that form the basis of any multimedia product, often doing so under very tight time constraints.

Content Developers

At some point, after the audio and video sources have been created but before the technology wizards have been summoned, there must be a person or group of people who assemble the actual content of a multimedia product. These brave souls venture into the world of copyright infringement and artist contracts, returning with the rights to publish the actual content that forms the basis of any multimedia title.

Content developers shoulder the burden of gathering all the multimedia pieces required for a given multimedia production. This might mean digging through half a million pieces of text, sorting out thousands of video clips and still images, and even hiring artists and technology wizards when needed. Content developers are similar in nature to television news producers: they assemble the various pieces of the final broadcast and do whatever it takes to get the job done under tight deadlines. They also drink lots of coffee and carry around plastic flasks full of pink antacid. It's a tough job.

Legal Eagles

Yes, indeed, the multimedia industry even has room for our friends in the legal world. After all, who is going to write all those contracts needed to procure the distribution and publishing rights to

author An individual who writes scripts, which form the core piece of content from which other content is developed. The author has full creative reign, just as the author of an original book or movie sript has. The author invents and develops the plot, characters, and story line.

script Created by an author (or number of authors), the idea or concept in written form is called a script, and is the backbone of the entire multimedia product.

video clips, photography, drawing, and prose? Eagle-eyed lawyers who don't miss a beat when it comes to multimedia contract details, of course!

The legal industry is rife with activity in the multimedia area, not only in the drawing up of contracts but also in the lawsuit arena. Everyone needs a good lawyer to begin with, and the multimedia industry ushers in a whole new world of legal issues with which to contend. Legally obtaining the rights to video and audio sources for multimedia products is just the tip of the iceberg. The legal world is every bit as excited and involved with the multimedia revolution as you and I are, if only for different, perhaps more lucrative, reasons.

Authors

Superb multimedia products don't simply materialize out of thin air, despite the best efforts of technology wizards and content developers. Before most multimedia products see the light of day, they often begin as the spark of creativity ignited in the mind of an *author.* Just as the film, television, and radio industries rely on authors to write the *script* and develop the plot, so too does the multimedia industry.

Boatloads of artists, technology wizards, content developers, and multimedia studios would be adrift at sea without a script and plot to reel them in. The backbone of any multimedia product, the script, pulls everyone together and gives them direction and purpose. Plot pulls consumers in and keeps them hooked. And without the author, neither of these are possible.

Take for instance the *Otherselves: The World In The Christmas Tree* multimedia product, which is now under development. Originating as a literary work, the *Otherselves* story was the basis of a multimedia production that pulled together the talents of artists, content developers, and technology wizards, giving each party direction and purpose. Without the original story line, the full-blown multimedia product would never have been possible, let alone conceived.

Although the *Otherselves* saga was written by a single author, many multimedia products involve the skills of multiple authors. Many products are translated into foreign languages, requiring a number of authors to convert the original work into different languages while preserving the power, intent, and integrity of the original work. And just as the computer has opened up a world of possibilities for artists, the multimedia author must rise to the challenge of writing scripts and plots that take into account the interactive nature of the technology. Multimedia breaks the barriers of our linear world, especially when it comes to literature. Hang on tight as authors tightly embrace and squeeze every ounce of power from hypertext and hypermedia prose and plot development; the ride has just begun.

```
▭▭▭▭      Otherselves-The World In The...      ▭▭
                    OTHERSELVES
           THE WORLD IN THE CHRISTMAS TREE
                Copyright 1995 by Tim Walsh

                       PART TWO
         The tiny band had safely crossed the harsh Plain of
    Cema.  They had traveled rapidly, their spirits and energy
    high, skirting vast stretches of the flat, rock-hard surface
    of the Plain, where the early wind had blown the snow clear.
    In order for Daling's red glass sleigh to move easily they
    had stayed in the loose, shallow snow the wind had left at
    the edges of the bare open areas.
         Now the eight Otherselves stood at the lip of the Double
    Ledges of Cema, looking down a long ridge of drifted snow.
    This, the north end of the Double Ledges, looked like a
    sharply declining mountainside.  Near the lowest ridge, where
    it joined the more nearly flat surface of the Plain of Bakya,
    they could see the huge wheel of a tipped over Sameself
    child's tricycle turning slowly in occasional wisps of night
    wind.
         "I made enough rope from spiderweb to lower Daling and
    the sleigh from ledge to ledge," said Paj.  "But maybe we can
    chance sliding down the mountainside."
         "Would it be too dangerous to slide?" asked Feetee.  She
    had great trust in the strength and intelligence of her
    husband, Paj, knowing he liked nothing better than to pit his
    enormous strength and endurance against some great task.  But
    Page 10              ◄◄►►◄ Normal+...        ◄        ►► ▭
```

▶ *Multimedia products start out as an original idea or concept long before the actual software development begins. Authors then turn the concept into a script, upon which the full-blown production is based. This script is for* Otherselves: The World In The Christmas Tree, *a multimedia product now under development.*

Actors

You know multimedia is a revolution here to stay when Hollywood's Screen Actors Guild forms the Interactive Media division! Yes, there is even room for actors and actresses.

▶ *The* Wing Commander *series of entertainment products squeezes every bit of performance out of today's multimedia technology.*

Hollywood knows multimedia isn't a passing fad, and it sits on the cutting edge of technology when it comes to exploiting the talents of its talent. Disney has recently released multimedia products based on their blockbuster hits *Aladdin* and *The Lion King.* Even George Lucas of *Star Wars* fame has stepped up to bat, forming LucasArts multimedia entertainment. But perhaps the most extensive interactive multimedia computer product to reach the market this year will come from Origin Systems Incorporated. Due in late 1995, its most recent product, *Wing Commander IV: The Price of Freedom,* spans four CD-ROMs, features actors Mark Hamill (*Star Wars*) and Malcolm McDowell (*A Clockwork Orange*), and has cost in excess of $4 million to create.

Wing Commander IV isn't the first multimedia product to employ real actors, and it's only a hint of things to come. With Dream-Works SDK well under way and many other Hollywood studios racing to bring the next killer entertainment product to market, multimedia actors and actresses are in great demand. It won't be long before standard Hollywood contracts include clauses specifically designed to address the multimedia aspects of the acting business, courtesy of technology-savvy lawyers and business-minded film executives.

Producers

Any undertaking as complex and difficult as multimedia requires the constant attention of a producer. In contrast to their Hollywood counterparts, multimedia *producers* not only manage thespians, artists and sound crews, but must also keep technology wizards, scriptwriters, and lawyers on track.

Multimedia producers exemplify the need for industrial-strength antacids and 'round-the-clock stress management support groups. With multimedia productions swiftly closing in on Hollywood movies in terms of budget, casting and legal demands, while coupled with incredibly complicated technology issues and an exploding market demand, multimedia producers work in a frenzy of excitement and exhaustion.

There are, of course, less-demanding producing jobs in the multimedia industry. Not everyone works under tremendous stress and time constraints, as there is an almost limitless number of unique multimedia products now under development that require varying levels of intensity from a producer. Producers can find projects that match their skills, ensuring a healthy mind and body when the final product ships.

producers Individuals who manage all aspects of multimedia projects, including overseeing actors, artists, sound crews, technology wizards, scriptwriters, and lawyers involved in the projects.

interactive movies Full-motion, full-color movies we can truly be part of. Delivered on CD-ROM or over the Internet, the interactive multimedia movie requires state-of-the-art hardware and software to be truly realistic.

Educators

One of the fastest growing segments of the multimedia industry is the educational market, which includes edutainment products designed to make learning fun. While these products require all the skill and talent of standard multimedia titles during their development, they also require a solid base of education on which to build.

Educators have contributed tremendously to the multimedia revolution, and in many instances provide the inspiration and initial groundwork for commercial multimedia products. Several edutainment products now on store shelves began as the personal project of a teacher determined to educate his or her students in the most effective way possible, while some of the very best multimedia

▶ *Children develop deductive reasoning skills, reading comprehension skills, and a keen interest in literature, when they play Brøderbund's* Alien Tales.

in existence lives anonymously in research labs and classrooms across the country. Many of the later products will never make it into the public eye, for the simple reason that most educators aren't in it for the fame and money but for the good of their students.

Musicians

A different discipline than sound engineering altogether, the music industry has recently leapt feet first into the multimedia waters, with David Bowie, Peter Gabriel, and Billy Idol taking the first plunge. Multimedia delivers what MTV has long known: When images are set in motion to the beat of music, the world will watch and listen as if in a trance. But multimedia gives the world what television never could — interactivity.

Music industry veteran Peter Gabriel apparently understands the implications of multimedia music, having recently released an interactive CD-ROM that lets users not only listen to his music but also participate in the process. Watch, listen, and arrange musical compositions and video effects yourself, all from the comfort of your personal computer. Gabriel knows this is the wave of the future and has formed his own interactive multimedia company to keep him in the forefront of multimedia and music technology.

The days of coffee shop jazz bands and mosh-pit rock 'n' rollers aren't over; they are simply changing with the times. Ch-ch-ch changes, as Bowie would say. Even veterans like Aerosmith have taken the plunge, along with Madonna, making some of their newest tunes available in cyberspace before they even hit the music store shelves. With established musicians as well as new voices on the scene getting plugged into the interactive world, we can expect some fantastic multimedia products from the music industry in the near future.

Hackers

hacker Counterculture heroes who develop software products and occasionally break into sensitive information systems for the sheer joy of discovery.

If there is an antithesis to the big-bucks, large-scale multimedia production studio, it is the *hacker.* Hackers are counterculture heroes who develop software products and occasionally break into sensitive information systems for the sheer joy of discovery. They are, at heart, pure in their intent. They live to create, explore, and share. Without hackers, the personal computer wouldn't have seen the light of day as early as it did and certainly wouldn't have evolved so rapidly.

Hackers are a unique combination of authoring wizard, software engineer, artist, and visionary, pursuing their craft with unbridled passion and drive. Usually working from home or at school while fueled by caffeine and sugary treats, these night owls attack each new technology challenge with gusto and tenacity, and are largely responsible for advancing the state of the art and making the personal computer industry what it is today.

Keep your eyes peeled for innovative products developed by small, no-name companies and individuals, for they often bring the most significant contributions to technology and the arts, as those fueled by an intense desire to create and learn often do. And while many hackers work alone, or in small groups, many can be found behind the scenes in major productions. Hackers exist at all levels of the industry, and can't be thanked enough for their contribution to the world of technology. Just ask Bill Gates, Apple Computer, and an entire generation of hippies.

PART 6

Getting into Multimedia

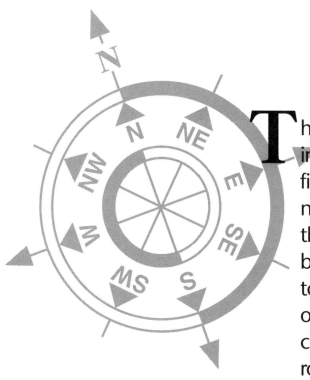

The career possibilities in the multimedia field are nearly as numerous as the titles themselves and can be every bit as difficult to decide on because of the wide array of choices. To help narrow the field a bit, let's take a look at some of the key areas for career opportunities and how to get the training you'll need. Also, let's peer into the future and see where you might position yourself for future success in this rapidly growing industry.

Career Choices in Multimedia

Since you are reading this book to become familiar with multimedia in the first place, I'll make the perhaps inaccurate assumption that you are not already in the industry to begin with. And since most software and hardware engineers already know about multimedia, I'll further assume that any interest you have in multimedia from a technological standpoint stems from a desire to author, or create, multimedia products yourself. Therefore, I won't advise existing software and hardware engineers on how to get into multimedia but will instead describe how you can get in on the authoring side of multimedia without first obtaining an engineering degree. Sound fair?

▶ *If you enjoy using multimedia products, you might want to take a crack at creating such products as well. (from Creative Multimedia's* The Masters)

I'll also assume you're not an actor or actress, since I haven't met many of these professionals in my life and couldn't adequately advise them on getting into the multimedia industry beyond suggesting they join the Screen Actors Guild's Interactive Media division and begin pushing their agents to find them multimedia acting roles.

The areas mentioned in here are more or less the key areas in multimedia — places where you are likely to find a good deal of employment opportunity. Each career area assumes an existing base of experience in that particular area, and so you are unlikely to fall into one of these careers without first spending some time developing the needed skills. Later in this part of the book, you'll find some information on multimedia training to help you obtain and polish your skills.

artists Creators of artwork needed for multimedia titles. Some create backgrounds, others design entire scenes.

Artists

If you have some degree of artistic talent, whether using the computer or more traditional tools such as paintbrush and canvas, pen and ink, or even spray paint on city walls, you may find the multimedia industry a perfect match for your skills.

A wide range of *artists* work in the multimedia industry. Some create backgrounds for multimedia movies and other visually oriented products, while others design entire scenes. The tools multimedia artists rely on range from standard painting and drawing software products to highly sophisticated 3-D modeling and animation products. Given the wide range of original artwork required for most multimedia products, you are likely to find an area to match your skills. Science

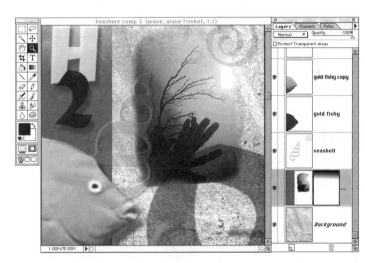

▶ *Adobe's* Photoshop *is one of the more popular tools used by a wide range of computer artists.*

sound engineers
People involved with sound in multimedia apply skills found in the traditional sound industry (such as recording and editing, dubbing, or generating audio effects, to name a few) to the highly technical field of computerized sound.

fiction, fantasy, psychedelic, and children's artwork are but a few of the popular categories in the multimedia art world.

Sound Engineers

If you already have experience in the sound industry or even in the recording studio, whether creating sound effects for movies or dubbing videotapes and manipulating audio sound tracks, you will find the multimedia industry an exciting and challenging place to work.

People involved with sound in multimedia apply skills found in the traditional sound industry (such as recording and editing, dubbing, or generating audio effects, to name a few) to the highly technical field of computerized sound. These folks, who often sport the intimidating job title of *sound engineer*, are responsible for the audio content of the multimedia products they help develop.

▶ *Artists create the realistic images you'll see in most of today's edutainment programs. (from MECC's* Oregon Trail)

In some cases their work is fairly straightforward, involving such routine work as converting or recording a traditional sound or musical work into a format the computer can understand. More often, however, they must dig deep into their repertoire of computer software and deeper still into their vast knowledge of the traditional and electronic sound worlds, spending long hours hunting down the tricky and elusive problems that often occur when sound is part of a multimedia product. The source of every strange hiss, pop, stutter, or skip must be located and resolved by the sound engineer, ensuring that the final product ships with the highest quality audio content possible.

Authoring Wizards

Do you enjoy using state-of-the-art software and hardware tools, while creating something people have never seen before? If you're comfortable learning and using new and complicated software products as they hit the market, then authoring multimedia products may be right up your alley.

Authoring wizards start each new product with a multimedia script, a ton of multimedia content stored on a high-capacity hard drive in no particular order, and a computer loaded with multimedia authoring tools and high performance hardware. From these, the authoring wizard must develop multimedia titles under rigid specifications for how the end product will look and perform, and under even more stringent, sometimes impossible, deadlines.

While authoring wizards typically possess a great deal of their own creative talent, which is expressed in the products they develop, they must also work within the guidelines and specifications supplied by their

authoring wizards
Individuals who develop multimedia titles under rigid specifications for how the end product will look and perform, and under even more stringent, sometimes impossible, deadlines. They start each new product with a multimedia script, a ton of multimedia content stored on a high-capacity hard drive in no particular order, and a computer loaded with multimedia authoring tools and high performance hardware.

▶ *Sound effects are an important part of all multimedia programs, especially action titles such as Origin's* BioForge.

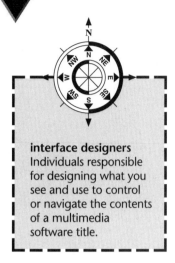

interface designers
Individuals responsible for designing what you see and use to control or navigate the contents of a multimedia software title.

employer. Regular evaluations of, and changes to, products under development result in the need for constant refinements and alterations that the authoring wizard must perform until the employer or customer is satisfied.

Although developing products that are constantly changing can be frustrating, it comes with the territory. In the end, however, authoring wizards can beam with pride when they walk into a computer store or open up a software catalog and point to the product they gave life to. And, as with any creative undertaking, the process is exhilarating and the end result infinitely gratifying.

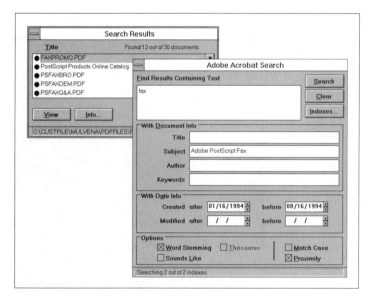

▶ With Adobe Acrobat, *novice and professional authoring wizards alike can create impressive hypertext and hypermedia multimedia products with ease.*

Interface Designers

The work of the best *interface designers* is rarely noticed. If the interface to a multimedia product is designed well, you'll navigate the contents with ease and have little difficulty understanding the controls to do so. Poorly designed interfaces, however, make the user painfully aware of the inadequate navigation controls or interface in general. In short, the interface designer is responsible for designing what you see and use to control or navigate the contents of a title.

Don't be fooled by the simplistic definition of interface design. The sheer volume of information and complex content of any multimedia product, the body of that product, must somehow be accessible to the user in a manner that is simple to learn and use, yet at the same time is unobtrusive and powerful in capability. Every detail must be considered and designed with this requirement in mind. And each degree of multimedia demands a unique interface.

It wouldn't make sense for a reference guide on home repair to use a video game interface, or vice versa. Every control, button, menu, and interface element must be designed with the user

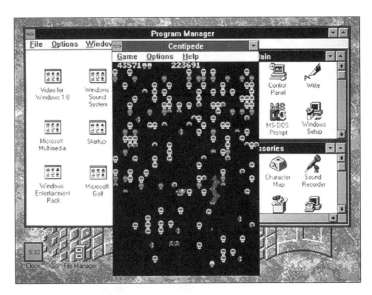

▶ *Interface designers work hard to keep multimedia products simple to learn and use.*

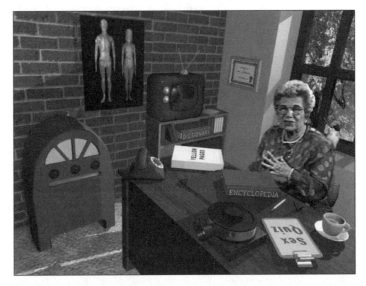

▶ *The interface for a reference product needs to be designed with the user and content in mind. (from Creative Multimedia's* Dr. Ruth's Encyclopedia of Sex)

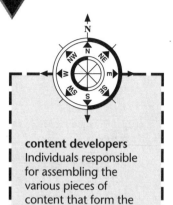

content developers
Individuals responsible for assembling the various pieces of content that form the basis of any multimedia product, often doing so under very tight time constraints.

and content in mind. Attention must be paid at every level to the way in which humans interact with computers and specific product contents, even down to age groups and gender. If a particular product is targeted toward young girls in their preteens, the required interface is quite different than that needed to capture and keep the attention of teenage boys. Not only must the content itself be considered, but a particular interface appropriate for the target audience must be employed if the product is to succeed.

These are just a few of the details interface designers worry about, and the best in the business know how to match the user and content with an appropriate interface. While the best designed interfaces in the real world go unnoticed, such as the shoelace or car door, those that fall short of the mark are cursed daily by those who must use them. The same is true for the multimedia industry; it takes a lot of work to make something easy to use.

▶ *Content developers must pull together every source of content in a multimedia project, including that contributed by artists, actors, animators, musicians, and authors. (from Origin's* Wings of Glory)

Content Developers

Multimedia *content developers* are very similar to producers in the news industry. They are responsible for assembling the various pieces of content that form the basis of any multimedia product, and often do so under very tight time constraints.

Content developers are essentially information sponges that take a *Rambo*-like approach to finding and gathering media sources. They absorb everything they read, see, and hear.

When the script for a multimedia product is dropped on their desks, these data warriors hunt down every last stitch of media that even remotely relates to the project.

If content isn't already available to which they can obtain the usage and distribution rights through legal contracts, content developers will often arrange for custom content development. During this stage of their information treasure hunt, content developers hire and direct whomever is needed for the job. Artists, actors, animators, musicians, and authors are but a few of the people content developers must pull together to extract quality work from under stringent deadlines.

author An individual who writes scripts, which form the core piece of content from which other content is developed.

script Created by an author (or number or authors), the idea or concept in written form is called a script, and is the backbone of the entire multimedia product.

Being a content developer isn't for everyone. It's a tough job, requiring a very special mix of intellect, long-term memory, and short-term crisis management skills. Good content developers are constantly on the lookout for material they might use in current and future products, and so they remember each piece of content they come across, no matter how insignificant it may seem. When deadlines approach, the best of the bunch handle the stress with apparent ease, ensuring their content is delivered on time. This often means the content developer must juggle several tasks at once to get the job done, from finding and assembling the content, to negotiating the right to utilize content owned by others, to handling the production of original content. In the end, however, a good content developer manages to get the job done where others might fail.

Authors

In many multimedia products, such as interactive movies and electronic literature, an *author* writes an original piece of work, often called a *script,* which forms the core piece of content from which

user group A small, privately run computer support organization devoted to the study of, and sharing of, information related to software and/or hardware.

▶ *Save yourself time and money by doing a little research on those flashy multimedia training programs often advertised through direct mail fliers before you attend. A good place to start is your user group, where you'll often find other members who have first-hand experience with these programs.*

other content is developed. Here, the author has full creative reign, just as the author of an original book or movie script has. The author invents and develops the plot, characters, and storyline.

Some multimedia authors, however, do not write the original literary work from which a product springs. In many instances, authors are called upon by content developers to contribute a piece of writing that is only one small piece of a much larger product. These authors are similar to authors who write newspaper columns or do research for magazines and reference manuals. In this case, many authors may be called upon to contribute their individual skills to a group effort, often a reference or informational product.

Microsoft's Encarta product is a good example of this practice, in which a number of talented authors contributed to this multimedia encyclopedia. Each author received credit for his or her work, and the final product is extremely rich in depth and breadth, thanks to the combined efforts of many writers and content contributors.

A Caveat on Training Programs

Just as multimedia has exploded onto the scene, so too has the number of training programs that promise to carry you over the cutting edge of technology. It seems that every few days I receive a piece or two of very colorful literature describing multimedia training programs guaranteed to give me the competitive edge in this fast-moving industry. Most of the stuff is incredibly attractive garbage, though, and you can save yourself thousands of dollars by putting it where it belongs — in the trash.

Be very wary of multimedia training programs that promise you the world for the price of a used car. You would almost always get more mileage from the car. Not all multimedia training programs are a waste of time and money, of course, but many are. If you are serious about getting into multimedia, you need to start in the right place. In fact, even if you have no interest whatsoever in the multimedia business but simply want to get the most out of your multimedia products or computer, you can save a lot of money, heartache, and frustration by immediately becoming a member of a good user group.

Getting the Most Out of User Groups

▶ *Berkeley Mac User Group (BMUG) maintains its own on-line service, also known as an electronic bulletin board system (BBS), to keep the lines of communication open with its members.*

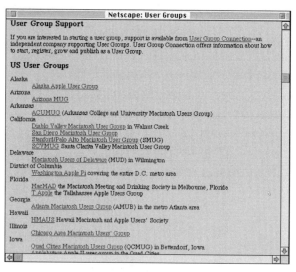

▶ *The Internet is an excellent source for all types of computer-related information. This list of United States user groups was found on the Internet and is updated regularly.*

I can't rave enough about the value of joining a good *user group*. These small, privately run computer support organizations are as vital to the new computer user as a good public relations director is to a politician: they can brighten your outlook on everything and make you look good in the process.

User Group Basics

User groups are everywhere it seems, each having a specific purpose in life. There are large, all-encompassing groups such as the Boston Computer Society (BCS), which provide top-notch advice, support, and training on nearly every level of computing and software imaginable.

Then there are smaller, more highly focused groups that may be nothing more than a handful of people who get together regularly to learn, discuss, and share things of interest for the benefit of their members. These latter groups generally tend to have informal names, since they don't have to worry about attracting and retaining a large base of members. My favorite of these is the MacPigs User Group, based in North Dakota. As you can probably gather from the name, MacPigs focuses on the Macintosh and has formed its user group in order to get the most out of its beloved computers and software. As for the second part of the group's name, I can only guess at its meaning. But, just to be on the safe side, you can be sure I'll never attend its annual barbecue.

The point is, if you have a computer (or need advice on buying one), you should seriously consider joining a user group. There are groups of all sizes and flavors. There is certain to be a user group in your state that matches your interests. And before you spend a single dollar on multimedia training, you should know that a good user group will often give you the best training around for a fraction of the price. The average user group provides an amazing amount of training to members for free, with annual dues rarely exceeding $50. In contrast, the typical three- to four-day multimedia training program can cost anywhere from $250 to $1,500!

User Groups as Training Resources

User group members also have a very different approach toward training and technology in general. Where commercial training programs are designed to generate profit, the typical user group shares information with whomever is interested. User groups consist of the most fascinating mix of people you're likely to see gathered to-gether in one room, yet all share the same interests in technology as you do. They exchange information for the sheer joy of sharing, not for profit. Because user group staff and volunteers are driven to use com-puter technology by a passion and are not motivated by a paycheck, you can be assured you'll get some of the best advice and training available without paying through the nose for it.

▶ *Although many user groups supply members with access to their own on-line services, others use a commercial on-line service. Available through eWorld, Apple Computer's commercial on-line service, the User Group Connection, is an organization that offers software and hard-ware discounts to anyone who is a member of a user group in the U.S.*

Multimedia Connections Through User Groups

Many multimedia professionals already in the business belong to user groups, giving you a chance to get the inside scoop on the industry without wasting valuable time and cash. Remember, for the most part, both user group staff and members like to talk about computers and will answer your questions and suggest places to get the professional training you may eventually need.

Many user groups keep a regular calendar of events and meetings, giving you a chance to join the festivities on your own schedule. And while you may initially be the one asking questions, in no time you'll also find yourself answering questions asked by fellow members. User groups are a unique combination of individuals who delight in sharing information, which you'll soon find yourself contributing to. They also provide an opportunity and an excuse to socialize, which everyone needs a bit of from time to time.

Finding a Good User Group

So how do you know if a group is any good? First you must decide on what it is you need from the group, and then determine if the group provides it at a price within your reach.

Asking the key questions

In the case of multimedia, you're almost certain to find that every user group in your area sets aside special meetings and even training to dedicate to this hot topic, but you'll also want to find out just how much multimedia they really offer. In addition, there are some general questions you should ask when you're shopping around for a user group:

- Do the members simply get together occasionally to discuss the technology as a casual interest, or are there regular events you can count on?

- Does the user group publish a newsletter or a calendar of events? If not, you may want to look elsewhere. Any group that doesn't have the resources to publish a newsletter or calendar of events, either on paper or in computer form such as electronic mail, probably doesn't have the resources to give you substantial support and training in the multimedia arena.

- Do they allow you to test drive software (or do they have a software library you can use)? A big perk of many larger user groups is their ability to gather some of the most current and sophisticated products on the market, allowing you to test drive them before spending the money yourself.

The Boston Computer Society has what it calls the Resource Center, where you can walk in and pick nearly any product you could want off the shelf and try it out. This is the perfect place to become familiar with some of the more expensive multimedia products on the market, and there is always someone within earshot to help out when you need it. The idea is that you'll use the Resource Center to evaluate a product before spending big bucks, or even little bucks, on it.

▶ Most user groups publish a regular newsletter, keeping you abreast of new products and services in the rapidly evolving computer industry. Members often contribute to these publications, giving valuable, down-to-earth product reviews and recommendations.

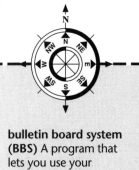

bulletin board system (BBS) A program that lets you use your personal computer to meet and correspond with others (for example, user group members) from the comfort of your home. You can also transfer files and send and receive messages through a BBS.

▶ Do they offer product reviews? Many user groups also publish product reviews written by their members. These aren't necessarily the polished and pretty reviews you'll see in industry magazines and journals, but they give you insights into how people like you or me might react to a particular product. Professional writers are usually just that: professionals.

User group members aren't always professionals in the computer industry, and so their experience with a product is often more down to earth and in line with what you might experience than that of the pros. These folks haven't spent their careers knee-deep in computer technology, and so they usually provide a more realistic perspective when it comes to reviewing software.

Ask prospective groups if they have product reviews, and also if you might contribute your own. Who knows, perhaps your first entry into the multimedia industry will come as a review of your own software published through your user group.

▶ Do they have an electronic *bulletin board system (BBS)*? One of the most valuable aspects of user groups is their ability to provide electronic access to their discussions, meetings, and members. Most groups maintain BBSs, which allow you to meet and correspond with members from the comfort of your home, using your personal computer.

If your user group doesn't have a BBS, you might ask why not. The ability to talk with others, hold meetings, and share a wealth of information such as product reviews, tip sheets, and late-breaking news, all without walking away from your computer, is an incredible benefit.

Many user groups publish their newsletters, event calendars, and training schedules on-line, so you can be up to date on everything the moment these items are composed. To make a good thing sound even better, many Bulletin Board Systems allow you to search for information using a keyword or set of keywords. Not only can you search for all published reviews of a particular product, but at the same time you might also search for all related events and training sessions in addition to every piece of correspondence ever written about the product by fellow group members. Can it get any better than this?

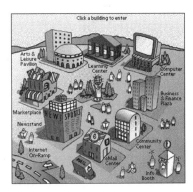

► *Welcome to eWorld! Apple Computer includes a free copy of its commercial on-line service software with every new Macintosh, giving users access to an exciting on-line community right out of the box. Technical support, software updates, industry journals, and magazines are just a few of the things Apple offers its customers through eWorld.*

While not every user group offers each of these benefits, you should ask about them anyway. If fact, some of these items may not appeal to you at all. But they are worth asking about, if only to get a feel for how well equipped the prospective group is. As with any product or service, you must figure out your own true requirements and then shop around for the best deal.

Two more questions

After you have determined if a user group offers what you need, you should find out two other key pieces of information needed to make a final decision:

▶ *How much* are the annual dues? Are training sessions extra, and if so, how much? How much support can you really expect once you've paid the dues, and are there any hidden costs or extra fees for anything?

▶ *How long* has the user group been around? If it hasn't been around for more than a few years, you might ask how long it's expected to be around. If the group is fairly new, how is it doing so far? Are there a lot of people you can expect to meet, or just a few?

In short, you want to ask the questions that will help you decide if joining the group is worth your time and money.

Once you have joined a good user group, take a few private moments to rejoice — you've found a valuable gem. Not only have you found a group of people interested in the same things you are, but you've found a source of some of the highest quality support and training around. As if that weren't enough, you may get the chance to test out software products before plunking down cash. And to boot you'll find that many groups offer the best pricing on software and hardware products anywhere you look, allowing you to buy the best products at the best prices. What a deal.

After spending some time getting into all the goodies that your new user group has to offer, you may find there is no need to pay for specialized multimedia training after all. But if you do decide that a commercial training program is something you'd like to pursue, you're certain to find people in your group who have either done it before or know somebody who has.

You'll find your group to be an invaluable resource when it comes to the best training programs in the multimedia industry, and you can trust their opinions because they have no financial motivation in sharing their experiences and thoughts. And because the industry changes so rapidly, your group will often provide better advice and feedback than journals and magazines, which require months of lead time to research products and training programs before they can go into print. Time and experience are of the essence in the multimedia industry, and your user group offers both.

All in all, a good user group can't be beat. Before you leap into expensive multimedia training, walk through the doors of your closest user group. You won't regret it.

Positioning Yourself in the Industry

If you are serious about getting into the multimedia business, then you'll also want to position yourself in the industry for the best future possible. Of course, your definition of a grand future is personal, and it may be different than that of others.

You may be searching for the most exciting job in the business to keep you on your toes, or perhaps you're looking for the most lucrative career path in the industry, or maybe even one that gives you the creative freedom you crave. Whatever your motives, you need to decide what it is you're ultimately looking for in a multimedia career and plan your moves accordingly.

Computer Industry Trends

It's impossible to predict with absolute certainty the trends and future hot spots of any industry, let alone one that moves as rapidly as multimedia. However, the very nature of multimedia dictates that there will be three key areas of sustained growth as this industry matures: audio, visual, and interactivity.

Also, there are specific trends that can be clearly seen looking back at computer technology as it has evolved over the past half century, making it a bit easier to forecast the future of multimedia with some degree of accuracy. Seeing and understanding the trends and hot spots of the computer industry in days gone by help us to map the future of multimedia for days to come. Looking back, there are three trends that become quite apparent when looking toward the future of multimedia:

▶ The computer industry is constantly and rapidly evolving. Computers are continually improving in speed, while becoming smaller in size and cheaper in price.

▶ Computer technology is finally becoming a consumer item. Computers and software are advertised on national television and can be bought at stores such as Sears and Wal-Mart. The age of computer technology as a consumer good is here.

▶ Computers are finally becoming standardized. There once was a time when each type of computer spoke its own unique language, was built from very specialized and highly *proprietary* hardware, and was incapable of sharing information with other computers without a heap of effort. With the help of rapidly improving technology and customer demand for machines that can talk to each other, the two key multimedia platforms, Macintosh and MS Windows, have finally reached a point where they can smoothly exchange information. It's about time.

The Future of Multimedia

Given the basic nature of multimedia, combined with hindsight when looking back in computing history, what can be expected in the near future of the industry? Where are the places for maximum career opportunity? And how can you ensure you won't become obsolete as everything else eventually becomes in the computer industry? While there are no absolutes, there are a few guidelines to follow.

Proprietary Kills

Never, ever, buy into proprietary computer hardware or software. By *proprietary* I mean any item that is designed to be used only by those who have express permission from the manufacturer. There used to be a time when proprietary stuff was the norm, since every computer manufacturer and software developer expected their specialized products to become wildly popular and eventually set the standard for that segment of the industry.

If a manufacturer held all the rights to a particular product, it could prohibit other manufacturers from using it or developing similar products. Then, if everything went the way they planned, people in the computer industry created such demand for their proprietary product that they could sell it at just about any price, because little or no competition existed. Better yet, they could make their product an industry standard by licensing the usage and distribution rights to other manufacturers. Since heavy demand was there, and manufacturers were prohibited from creating their own versions of the product, those who owned the rights could make a fortune from licensing deals alone.

Think for a moment if this happened in the world of pencils. Let's say, just for illustrative purposes, that the inventor of the first pencil eraser received a patent on it, thereby preventing others from creating or selling similar erasers. The inventor, Mr. Eraser-maker man, or Ms. Eraser-maker woman, as the case might be, could have become a wealthy person simply by allowing pencil makers to create their own erasers under license from the inventor. Or, the inventor of the eraser could have made a fortune by actually manufacturing the erasers and then selling them to the pencil makers. In fact, even bigger fortunes could be made by doing a little of both. Either

proprietary Any item that is designed to be used only by those who have express permission from the manufacturer.

▶ *One of the dangers of proprietary technology: If the industry doesn't fully embrace a proprietary technology and make it a standard, you'll often pay much more for a "one of a kind" product than it's worth.*

way, the person who held the rights to the eraser would be in for big bucks. This is the big appeal with proprietary products; when it's your invention, the world's your oyster. But there's also a downside to proprietary products, and the consumer usually shoulders this burden.

Suppose every other inventor at the time thought he would find fame and fortune by inventing the perfect, proprietary eraser. Every type of eraser you can imagine would be invented. Some of these products might sit on top of the pencil (like the ones we see today), and some would be handheld and not part of the pencil at all. These designs are OK, but in the mad scramble to create the perfect eraser without infringing on the proprietary rights of other eraser makers, a bizarre array of erasers would make it to market. Perhaps some would pierce the pencil itself, forming a cross from the writing instrument. How about an eraser that doubles as a fingergrip? It might be inconvenient to use, but it would get the job done. What about an eraser that looks exactly like a pencil, down to the lead in it? Why bother having wood pencils when rubber eraser pencils are available? Sure, they erase everything the moment you write it, but hey, some people would buy it, if only once.

The problem with proprietary products is that everyone has his own special way of doing things and nobody else can copy it without permission. The result is a world full of proprietary, inadequate products that are not only expensive but incapable of being intermingled without considerable effort. It can lead to a pretty ugly pencil.

The bottom line of this discussion of proprietary hardware and software is to make you aware of the danger of buying into a proprietary solution. Don't go for the bigger and better whiz-bang product unless you are certain it is compatible with existing standards. Stay clear of software that claims to have invented a new standard — if it's a new standard, you'll read about it in the trade magazines or at your user group meetings. Until then, keep away from those products that claim to break new ground unless you confirm that they work seamlessly and in concert with your existing setup, and are, in fact, worth the trouble of learning a new way of doing things altogether.

Cross Platform Compatibility

cross platform compatible Products that allow your work to move smoothly between Macintosh and Windows-based platforms.

Regardless of your career path (for example, as an artist, sound engineer, or authoring wizard) you want to ensure that your work can be shared among Macintosh and Windows computers. Since these systems make up the bulk of mainstream multimedia, to limit yourself to only one piece of the pie is a big mistake. This doesn't mean that you have to use both platforms, but it does mean you need to use products that allow your work to move smoothly between platforms.

The easiest way to ensure that your software products are *cross platform compatible* is to ask the following question *before* you buy anything: "Will I be able to share my files with both Macintosh and Windows users, and if so, what's the process?" While the answer may be yes, you'll also want to confirm that the product you are buying

▶ *Artwork created or edited in Adobe* Photoshop *can be used in any multimedia product, making this product a vital tool for many artists in the multimedia industry.*

is available for both platforms. Some products claim to be cross platform when they really only allow you to export your work in a format that can be used by other products, regardless of the platform.

Because you want to be as marketable and valued in the industry as possible, you should choose software products that are available on both Macintosh and Windows computers. This way you are able to work in either environment as needed and are much more flexible and, hence, more valuable in the multimedia industry. Stick with major software manufacturers whose business is focused on cross platform products.

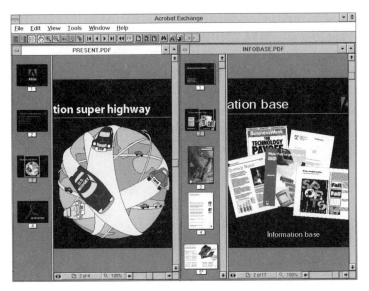

▶ *A major benefit of Adobe* Acrobat *is its ability to create cross platform products: when you create a product with Acrobat, regardless of which computer you use to do it, it can immediately be used on both Macintosh and Windows-based computers. This ability, often called Electronic Document Exchange, is extremely powerful and saves considerable time and effort on the part of authoring wizards.*

Microsoft, Adobe, Macromedia, and Fractal Design are a few of the larger companies dedicated to providing high quality cross platform software products. Just within these manufacturers you'll find the leading cross platform software products for artists, sound engineering, and authoring wizards.

Investing your money and time in cross platform products ensures that your work can be made available to both Macintosh and Windows worlds. This doesn't mean you should buy a copy of the product for each platform. Simply make sure that the product is an industry standard and available on both platforms. Then, purchase the product for whatever platform you use.

You'll spend considerable time and effort learning the ins and outs of any new product to begin with, and don't need to invest in both Macintosh and Windows systems to ensure you have the skills on both. Simply learn your new product as best you can; when you feel confident, test drive the same product on a new platform. This is something you might be able to do at your user group, but if not you can find other places to hone your cross platform skills.

Trade shows are a great place to sit down with your product's manufacturer and go over the finer points of the software, on either platform. If there's a trade show or convention coming to your area, give your software manufacturer a call and find out if it will be exhibiting its products, or if it knows of an exhibitor demonstrating its products who will let you take the controls for a while. If trade shows and conventions aren't up your alley, you can also return to the store where you bought the software and explain that you want to spend a little time testing the product you purchased there on a different platform. You spent a lot of money there if you bought any industry standard cross platform product, and so your vendor shouldn't have a problem letting you take the product for a spin on a different platform.

If all else fails, you can ask a friend or coworker who owns the software on a different platform it you can take a crack at it. You'll probably need a little help at first, since the Macintosh and Windows operating systems are quite different and can be confusing the first few times you move between them. However, you'll get the swing of it in no time and be applying your knowledge of the product almost immediately. Take the opportunity to put the product through its paces on the new platform. You may find that

bug A problem that prevents a software program from working properly or as expected.

version history A detailed listing that describes the various updates and fixes made on a software product from version to version.

some of the options your software supports are not available on this new platform, or are accessed in a very different way. You may even stumble upon some features your platform doesn't offer. Why is this?

Because software products are developed specifically for the hardware and operating system on which they will be used, they often feature capabilities unique to that platform. While there isn't much you can do about this, except learn the features supported on each platform, you do need to be certain your software versions are kept up to date if you want to keep current in the industry.

Features and Versions

Software is an evolving science. The very day a product is released to the public, software engineers are hard at work adding new capabilities and fixing problems (also known as *bugs*) the software might have. When these new features and bug fixes are in place and the software is deemed ready for public distribution, a new version of the product is released. Because software products typically undergo many changes during their lifetime, they generate what's known as a *version history*, a detailed listing that describes the various updates and fixes made from version to version.

For example, the software with which this book was written, Microsoft Word, has undergone multiple revisions since being released as version 1.0. It is now at version 6.0. Each new version of Microsoft Word fixed bugs found in the previous release, while adding a host of new features to make the upgrade fee palatable.

In order to keep yourself on the very tip of the multimedia iceberg, you must master each version of your software tools almost as soon as they are released. While the most current version available may not have features or bug fixes that appeal to you, they appeal to the industry. Nonprofessionals often skip a version or two of a product, since what they have gets the job done. However, industry professionals rely on their knowledge and skill of each software product in their repertoire of tools to stand out among the competition.

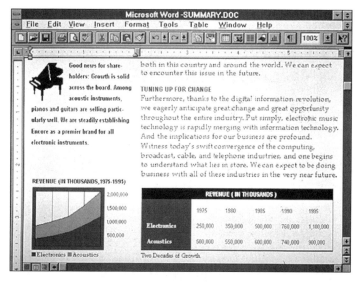

▶ One of the world's most popular word processing products, Microsoft Word, has evolved steadily over the years. The most current release, Microsoft Word Version 6.0, is infinitely more powerful than the first version, released many years ago.

Keeping your tools up to date, along with your skills for each tool, will give you the edge needed in the ultracompetitive multimedia field. It's simply not enough to know a product; you must know it inside and out and embrace each major version as it is released.

Sure, keeping up to date means money out of your pocket. If possible, have your employer purchase the upgrades regularly. If that's not an option, or if you are a freelancer, bite the bullet and pay for the upgrade yourself. When cash is tight, lean on your user group resources to test drive the most current versions until you can afford them yourself. To be a professional in this industry, you must find a way to keep your skills up to snuff. Once you are committed to upgrading your products, you'll notice just how fast the industry changes. Don't be surprised if each product you own is upgraded at least once a year, if not more often. It comes with the territory.

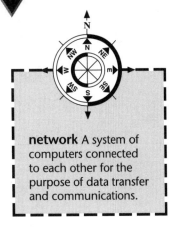

network A system of computers connected to each other for the purpose of data transfer and communications.

Networking Wonders

While you'll certainly gain valuable experience and a broad knowledge of your trade by doing a little old-fashioned elbow rubbing at user group meetings, trade shows, and conferences, this isn't the type of networking you'll need to stay afloat in the coming decades. Here we're talking about the physical connecting of computers, or *networks*, which allows them to communicate through phone wires and special cables.

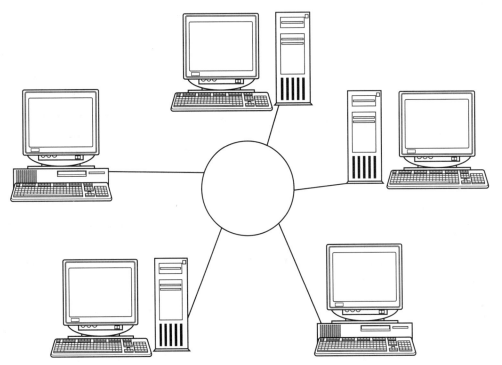

▶ *Networked computers are connected through specialized cables and/or standard telephone lines, making it possible to share information and communicate with one another. Networked computers are the backbone of the global Internet and commercial on-line services such as America Online, CompuServe, and Prodigy.*

The future of multimedia will be, without a doubt, networked content navigation. I mentioned earlier that the on-line arena was my personal favorite, and it will turn out to be one of the biggest areas of growth in the foreseeable future. This doesn't mean you need to learn how to set up a network yourself, but it does mean you need to keep a vigilant eye on the state of networked products and master the delivery of net-worked goods once your software tool becomes network savvy.

▶ *Commercial on-line services such as* America Online *give subscribers access to popular magazines.*

For instance, if you plan to be an authoring wizard, you'll also need to invest in tools that let you build multimedia products for networks. Here, multiple people can use your product instead of the single individual at a single computer. The same goes for anyone on the development side of the industry. If you are able to create networked, cross platform products, you'll be in demand.

Artists and authors should begin to look at techniques for creating works involving networked, multiuser access. There is a high level of complexity inherent here, and nobody knows exactly how the standards will evolve. You will, however, be at the crux of the industry if you begin developing your artwork or literature for networked access today.

If a project comes your way that features networked access, jump on it. All the experience you can get will help. Chances are it will become a nightmare at times, because there aren't many good examples of networked products to look at for help. However, you will be in at the ground level of the most pivotal revolution in computing we'll likely see: networked access to computer products and services, as opposed to individual access.

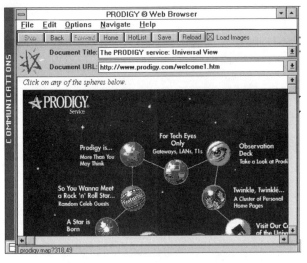

▶ *Prodigy allows users to browse the World Wide Web.*

If you haven't already joined an on-line service, now is the time. For sheer ease of use I suggest America Online. And, although more difficult to navigate than America Online, CompuServe and Prodigy have a tremendous amount of information and special multimedia discussion groups worth taking a look at. Each service comes with a free trial membership, so you can explore each to decide which is best for you before ponying up the monthly fees.

▶ *Keep abreast of industry news, stock prices, current events, and even your horoscope with CompuServe's Information Manager.*

Once you've decided, be sure to regularly attend on-line discussion groups and forums related to your multimedia tools, future technology, and networking. You'll be an extra step up on the technology ladder, often getting the inside scoop on changes happening in technology well before they reach the public, your customers, or your employer.

entertainment
Multimedia products designed to be used for pleasure, rather than learning purposes. Arcade, mystery, and adventure games are just a few examples of entertainment products.

Entertainment and Edutainment Explosions

Everyone loves entertainment, and what could be better than learning while you're having great fun? The use of multimedia in the entertainment and educational markets is exploding, and it's not going to slow down any time soon.

Look for strong growth in the entertainment field, whether as shoot-'em-up style video games or more subtle interactive entertainment products such as Myst or Gadget. Entertainment will always be a hot area, at least as long as people want to have fun. But also keep an eye on the

▶ *Entertainment titles like* Myst *will continue to be hot sellers.*

edutainment Educational multimedia products that not only teach but also entertain in the process. Learning with edutainment is a blast since you can have fun while being taught something. The best edutainment products make you forget you are learning.

emerging educational software products taking advantage of multimedia.

Edutainment is coming on strong, a rapidly growing market with no apparent end in sight. Multimedia promises to change the way we learn, and there are thousands of years of educational experiences just waiting to be combined with technology. Math, science, history, art, literature — you name it. If you can learn it, it can become an educational multimedia experience. And with the power of multimedia, it can also be turned into fun: edutainment.

For my money, there would be no hotter spot in the industry today than a good cross platform edutainment product that can be accessed by many people at once over a network. If you have a chance to work on something this exciting, don't pass it by. You'll be sorry if you do.

The Future of Multimedia

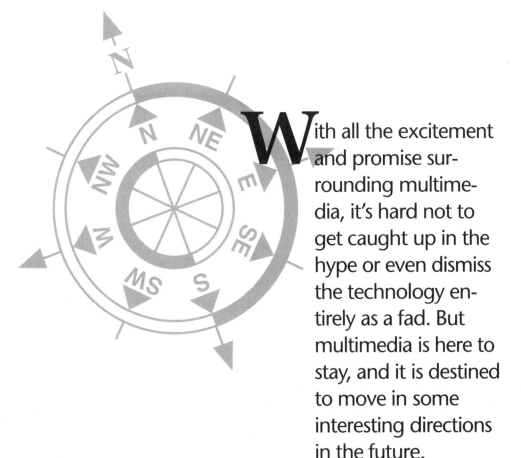

With all the excitement and promise surrounding multimedia, it's hard not to get caught up in the hype or even dismiss the technology entirely as a fad. But multimedia is here to stay, and it is destined to move in some interesting directions in the future.

Multimedia Is Here to Stay

Some mornings I wake up and expect the newspaper headlines to read "Multimedia a Big Hoax. Apple and Microsoft Claim It Was All in Good Fun." But after a fresh cup of coffee, a couple of hip-hugging exercises on my hula-hoop, and a dash of freeze-dried food for my precious pet rock, I assure myself that I'm no sucker and that this multimedia revolution is no fad.

Like any upstanding, law-abiding revolutionary, I need to know what I'm fighting for. Where is this all going, when will it be over, and how can I expense everything at the end of the coming fiscal year? We digital mercenaries must stagger through the daily rigors of this revolution, knee deep in cables and technical support sticky notes while engaged in hand-to-disk combat with incompatible equipment and poorly designed products. We look to the future for faith, strength, and confirmation that our efforts are not in vain.

And just what can we expect from multimedia in the near future? What types of products are being brewed up in research labs across the country, and what new equipment can multimedia revolutionaries expect to get their hands on soon? Furthermore, where is all this leading? Our forefathers of the American Revolution would never have believed that what we now take for granted would eventually come to be. Planes, trains, and automobiles. Microwave ovens, cellular phones, and fax machines. Broadway musicals,

▶ *Who could have predicted home computers a century ago, let alone multimedia? (from Electronic Arts Sports Basketball)*

movie theaters, and television sitcoms. And, of course, personal computers, interactivity, and multimedia. These are just a few of the things that were impossible to predict back then, yet have become part of our everyday life, and there will be just as many new and wonderful products to grow out of today's multimedia revolution.

Let's first take a look at what multimedia promises to deliver from an overall, general point of view. We'll then take a look at some of the more specific products and technologies coming down the pike, followed by a rousing look at the coming millennium and its relation to multimedia technology. Suit up, soldier, we're heading into the thick of things.

The Promise of Intellectual Freedom

Back in my day, we didn't have all these new-fangled conveniences of modern society. During the week, I walked three miles to school each day, where I was soundly whipped into intellectual shape by a stern schoolmaster. There was no library within walking distance, and when I eventually did get my hands on a book it was a treasure to behold. Back then, education was a privilege, and books were valuable treasures you would beg, borrow, or steal to get your hands on. We were grateful for every page of pulp and print, and often included Gutenberg in our daily prayers of thanks.

Well, okay. So maybe that was more like Abraham Lincoln's life, and not my own, but you get the point. Not too awfully long ago, education was indeed a privilege in which not everyone could participate. And only a select few could afford the luxury of exploring their personal interests for the sheer pleasure of satisfying intellectual curiosities.

►*Popular books are already available in multimedia form.*

Books were rare and expensive, and not everyone could get their hands on them, let alone gain access to hundreds of them in a public place such as a library or coffee shop. Information was passed down from generation to generation in printed form and story telling, with few feeling the true connection between education and entertainment. Those few who did often went on to become educators themselves, attempting to cultivate among their students a zest and enthusiasm for learning.

Educators at all levels passed on tried-and-true, time-honored learning devices, such as memorization, pop quizzes, and good old-fashioned peer pressure topped off with a dash of humiliation.

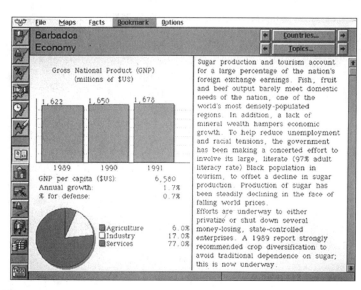

► *Multimedia products can help students learn history, geography, and economics.*

These educational techniques have remained essentially the same since the very first books were published, although modern-day courses are often fortified with video tapes and Cliffs notes.

While the days of reading, writing, and arithmetic aren't over by any stretch of the imagination, you can be sure multimedia is going to shake things up quite a bit. Look no further than your local computer superstore or mail-order multimedia catalog for proof. There seems to be no limit to the number of new multimedia products hitting the shelves, with a great deal of these targeted at the educational market place. Edutainment is an incredibly fast-growing segment of the multimedia market, with products now available to teach nearly every traditional discipline in a variety of new and creative ways. With multimedia, every one of us has the opportunity to explore our intellectual curiosity without even beginning to exhaust the supply of available material. In the whole scope of things, the single most important feature of multimedia is its ability to provide intellectual freedom while simultaneously providing an exciting and compelling entertainment experience.

But before we can truly break free of the constraints of today's educational system, there must be equality in terms of access. What good does multimedia do the masses when a few decent titles costs almost as much as the average person earns in an entire day? When this is the case, we are no better off than we were in the days of dear old Abe Lincoln: access to information remains a luxury in which only an elite group can indulge. Imagine rushing out to buy a half-dozen or so multimedia CD-ROMs to fully quench your thirst for a particular topic. Before the process of cerebral satisfaction could begin, you would have to shell out around $300 for the products. Now imagine paying

CD-ROM (Compact Disc Read Only Memory) A close relative to the audio Compact Disc we are all familiar with. CD-ROMs are able to store many types of media that may be accessed via computer. Because they are small and a massive amount of information may be stored on each disc, CD-ROM has become the most popular way of delivering multimedia to computer users.

▶ *Edutainment titles make basic math concepts fun to learn.*

World Wide Web A superset of the Internet that has been specially designed for visual access using special software known as a browser.

cyberspace A buzzword often used to describe the Internet or any of the commercial services available to consumers seeking access to the Net.

the Net Shorthand term used interchangeably with "the Internet."

information superhighway An analogy often used to describe the Internet, conjuring up images of long stretches of highway used to get from place to place fast.

this amount for every topic you want to explore. And this, of course, assumes you already have a well-equipped multimedia computer to begin with. Kind of takes the edge off your excitement, doesn't it? So much for equal intellectual freedom for all.

Sure, CD-ROMs will drop in price. They already have. But even if you are lucky enough to have a computer superstore down the street, or you buy your titles from a multimedia mail-order catalogue that delivers your purchases overnight, there is still a significant delay between your curiosity being piqued and it finally being satisfied. True, it's only a couple of days' wait or so assuming you know which titles you want, they are in stock, and you are willing to pay for them up front without knowing exactly what you're getting. But when it comes to intellectual freedom, every moment standing between you and the answers is nothing short of mental imprisonment. To truly be free in an information society, there must be no barriers between you and the answers you seek. Therefore, there must exist a higher road to intellectual freedom than simply CD-ROMs. And as luck would have it, there are many such roads.

The Promise of a Networked World

Cyberspace, the Internet, World Wide Web, Information Superhighway, the Net. Whatever you call it, this vast, globally networked community is fast becoming the wave of the future for communications and multimedia product delivery. Here, there is no wait. If you want something, you go onto the network and get it. Here, everything exists in networked computers, hard drives, and CD-ROM drives located around the world. Here, you have true intellectual freedom. Here, without a doubt, lies the future of multimedia and the road to intellectual freedom.

In the networked world, high-quality multimedia products and demos are only a click of the mouse away. Information databases abound, and your favorite publications are to be found faster than you can even hustle down to the mailbox or your corner newsstand. Using the networks, you truly get a feel for the power of information at your fingertips, and what is gained by true intellectual freedom. And as if the millions of products and services residing in cyberspace aren't enough, you'll be happy to know that the networked world isn't restricted to computer products and services. Here you can get direct access to real-world items as well. Order pizza, a cup of coffee, or flowers for your loved one with the click of a button.

Internet A vast, globally connected computer network developed by the United States government after World War II. Although originally designed to provide scientists and researchers with the ability to communicate using computers, the Internet has grown rapidly over the past decade to include a diverse group of approximately 30 million users world-wide.

Sure, you order things over the phone just as easily, but can you see the items before you buy them? In a networked world you can, and when appropriate you can hear them as well. Not only are true multimedia products available, but a few new inventions are appearing that really outshine their real-world counterparts. For example, several products have burst onto the scene that allow you to make a voice call over the network, to anywhere in the world, for the price of a local call.

Accessing the Internet

All of this is taking place on the *Internet,* a globally connected community of computers and users that has been around since World War II. But until lately, the Internet was the exclusive domain of researchers, educators, and computer hackers who not only

▶ *Popular magazines may now be read on-line, thanks to commercial on-line services such as America Online.*

▶ *Many commercial on-line services, such as CompuServe, provide access to the global Internet.*

had access to the system but also possessed the technical skills required to navigate a massive amount of information using nothing more than a textual interface.

All of that has changed, however, and now everyone can join in the digital dance. If you can navigate your computer, you can navigate the Internet. With the arrival of a graphical interface to its worldwide contents, cyberspace is as close as your home computer.

What Software Will You Need?

The easiest way to get onto the Internet is through a *commercial on-line service* provider such as America Online, CompuServe, or Prodigy. The more brave of heart can get a direct connection to the front lines of the digital revolution by hunting down a local Internet service provider. In this case you won't use the graphical interface supplied by a commercial service, but instead will use what's known as a *browser*. There are several browsers to choose from. Netscape (from Netscape Communications Corp.) is the most widely used. However you do it, get on the Net. There's something for everyone, and more fantastic information than you would be able to sort through in a multitude of lifetimes.

What Hardware Will You Need?

When you connect to the Internet, whether directly or through a commercial service provider, you'll do so through your existing phone line and a *modem* attached to your computer. The phone line is the physical cable over which information on the network travels, and the modem is the device that gets that data into your computer. For best results, you'll need a pretty fast modem. And just like CD-ROM drives, modems come in a variety of speeds, and faster is better. A slow modem will cripple your Internet cruising ability and eventually drive you mad. To avoid modem-triggered insanity, consult Appendix A before you buy one. I've lost many a friend to the slow-modem syndrome, and wouldn't wish that fate upon my worst enemy even during the midst of a digital revolution.

commercial on-line service Specialized on-line services provided by commercial companies such as America Online, Prodigy, and Compu-Serve. Commercial on-line services typically provide members with access to a multitude of software products, on-line discussion forums, technical support from a variety of vendors, and the ability to communicate using electronic mail (e-mail).

browser Specialized computer software that allows users to visually navigate the contents of the Internet by using a mouse. Without a browser, the Internet must be navigated using text commands entered through a computer keyboard.

modem A piece of hardware for connecting computers over telephone lines. Most personal computer users connect to the Internet over modems, although some have direct connections through company networks.

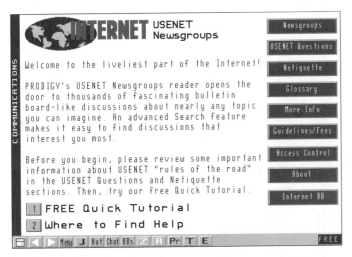

▶ *Internet content is as diverse as it is vast, with nearly all modern documents, correspondence, and software products available for the taking.*

How Much Will It Cost?

While the Internet is the best way to tap into the future and liberate your mind, it, as everything else, comes at a price. First, there is the basic cost of your multimedia computer. That's a given. Next, tack on the cost of a modem, which will run upwards of $100 for one fast enough to give you decent network cruising speeds. And finally, you'll get a kidney punch every month from your service provider. Whether using a commercial service or a direct Internet connection, expect to pay at least $15 per month to get decent use out of the Net. This is less than half the price of a typical CD-ROM title,

▶ With the World Wide Web, you can graphically navigate the Internet, provided you are using special "browser" software. Netscape is one of the most popular browsers available today. This browser makes it easy to navigate the Internet using hypertext and hypermedia.

▶ Computer hardware and software companies have found they are able to reduce technical support costs and improve customer relations using on-line services. Apple Computer, Inc., and Microsoft Corporation both have World Wide Web sites where users can get technical support if needed.

but still quite pricey when it comes to being affordable for everyone. For now, however, it's about the best way to get plugged into the future without losing your shirt. And, as we look even further into the future, products coming down the pike promise to make access to information even more affordable.

The Promise of Products on the Horizon

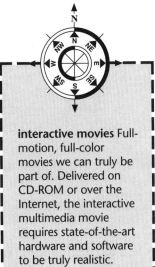

interactive movies Full-motion, full-color movies we can truly be part of. Delivered on CD-ROM or over the Internet, the interactive multimedia movie requires state-of-the-art hardware and software to be truly realistic.

Bigger, stronger, faster, and cheaper. Isn't that what the future always holds? Higher capacity hard drives and CD-ROM drives, stronger emphasis on well-designed multimedia products, and faster computer and phone lines are all in the works. With these will come the next generation of multimedia products, each bigger, stronger, and faster than those we have today. And, as multimedia technology steadily makes its way into the modern consumer's life, stiff competition and advances in technology promise to drive prices down, making it a little cheaper and less difficult to keep up with the times.

Interactive Movies

The first products to arrive on the scene exploiting the latest technological advances will most likely be truly *interactive movies.* Within the next few years we will see these full-motion, full-color movies delivered on CD-ROM and over the Internet. More than any other product, the interactive multimedia movie requires state-of-the-art hardware and software to be truly realistic. At about the time Hollywood begins to deliver its multimedia goods in mass, the high-powered technology needed to really get into the action will also become available.

virtual reality The ability to move about and control a multimedia experience from your own perspective and as a full participant rather than a passive viewer.

Virtual Reality

Expect *virtual reality* (*VR*) to finally become a reality at around the same time truly interactive movies hit the scene. This much ballyhooed technology simply hasn't lived up to the hype, for many reasons, mostly technological. Within a few years, however, expect the technology issues now prohibiting VR from hitting the mainstream to be resolved, at which point it will truly blossom.

With virtual reality, you'll not only be able to interact with multimedia movies, but you'll believe you are actually part of them. For the best effect, you'll likely don a set of video goggles, each eyepiece of which will display a slightly altered version of the same image. The result will be nothing less than mind shattering, as you walk, run, leap, and dive into realistic 3-D experiences. The hardware and software to do this is just now beginning to become available at a somewhat reasonable price and with acceptable performance. In about two years it should hit full force, at which point you may want to consider a health care plan that covers you in the event of a virtual accident.

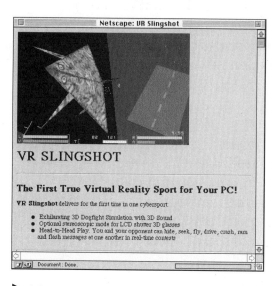

▶ *Many commercial software products can be found on the Internet. This game, VR Slingshot, was found advertised on the World Wide Web.*

Multimedia Sounds Abound

But vast improvements in the visual domain aren't the only advances coming down the multimedia pike. Eventually audio will become better integrated into multimedia software products, as the traditional music industry finally embraces multimedia technology. Led by pioneers of today such as Peter Gabriel, David Bowie, Billy Idol, and Todd Rundgren, tomorrow's music and images will eventually converge into one, and in time you'll rarely experience one without the other. Of course you'll usually have the option of listening to music without the accompanying images, but you'll generally find the combination of the two overwhelmingly more enjoyable than experiencing them independently. Either way, expect high-fidelity, stereo sound tracks to come standard with most multimedia products.

Although there are simply too many constraints with today's technology to cram over one hour of decent video and sound onto a single CD-ROM, give it time. Within three years the capacity of CD-ROMs will be significantly greater than those we have today, and with high-grade compression and decompression technology they'll be fast enough to play full-motion video and stereo sound all while providing the interaction we expect from multimedia. Computer systems themselves will keep pace, if not lead the race, being powerful enough to deliver the final product smoothly and with realism you wouldn't believe possible looking at today's products.

> **MIDI (Musical Instrument Digital Interface)** A specialized music technology, typically a combination of specialized hardware and software, that provides the ability to record and/or playback musical instruments using the computer. MIDI music is very different from computerized digital audio sources, which is an actual recording of music, whereas MIDI is similar to sheet music that is used to command different musical instruments.

Audio and Video Take the Lead

With the arrival of new and incredibly powerful personal computers, advanced graphics technology, and fully integrated music and sound, text will soon become reserved for information that isn't easily conveyed using sounds or images. Just like television and movies, audio and video will become the main sources of multimedia content. Text will still exist, yet become less and less of a focal point. Presently, text is the easiest media type to create and navigate with a multimedia product. In less than five years, however,

hypertext A system that links words and phrases together so you can navigate textual information in a free-form fashion that is faster and more accurate than other methods of searching for information.

hypermedia A system that uses the same principles found with hypertext. Photographs, video, sound, and text can be linked to one another to form a system of interconnected media. With hypermedia, just as with hypertext, you are able to navigate information in a free-form manner that fits your style and needs. Hypermedia, however, delivers a wealth of visual and audible material that cannot be achieved by text alone.

you or I will be able to create and distribute sophisticated multimedia products with about the same difficulty as we now have using a word processor.

Don't believe it? Did you ever think you'd be able to make home videos by simply pointing a video camera and pressing a button? In time you'll be able to do the same, yet the resulting images and sounds will wind up on your computer instead of a video tape. This technology is already available, and will in time become relatively inexpensive and easy enough to use that you won't think twice about sending your photographs, videos, and voice recordings to friends and relatives through the Net. Typing a letter will seem a bit old fashioned, since we can talk much faster than we can type.

Although text will never disappear altogether, future technology advances will allow everyone to easily communicate using images and sound instead. As a result, textual information will become less of a focus in nonreference multimedia products. If a picture is worth a thousand words, and a movie worth a million, how many words is a word worth?

Do-It-Yourself Multimedia

These advances in multimedia technology will usher in a new world of multimedia products, limited only by the imagination of their creators. While cream-of-the-crop multimedia products will still cost an arm and a leg to produce, future technological advances will make it possible for everyone to create products of their very own. If you can point a camera and use a computer, you'll be able to create your own multimedia products. Whether these products are entertainment, educational, or simply reference, we'll be doing it ourselves before ringing in the new millennium, probably without even realizing it.

Remember, if a product contains more than a single source of media and provides interaction, it's multimedia. And as it becomes easier and easier to assemble text, video, and sound on our home computers, we'll become multimedia authors ourselves. The products we create may not be intended for public consumption, perhaps being as personal as interactive albums containing photos, video, and audio recordings of family vacations, birthdays, and similar events, but they will be multimedia nonetheless.

The Promise of New Technologies Now upon Us

While all of these exiting new products heading towards us may seem like they are far off in the distance, there are many technologies already on the market that point to the future of multimedia and true intellectual freedom.

Current Connections

To begin with, I suspect modems as we know them will eventually be replaced by computers that have built-in, cable-ready capabilities. The television, as we now know it, will become as antiquated as silent pictures and the jukebox are today. By the year 2000 new technologies now on the horizon will have arrived, matured, and changed the way we look at everything, from daily news to Hollywood movies to friends and family. Not only will we be viewing things in a different way,

▶ *Multimedia changes the way we receive the day's news headlines.*

we'll be interacting with them as well. Move over, Rover, there's a new dog coming to town with a whole new bag of tricks in its jaws.

But before jumping too far into the future, let's take a look at what's going on today that might help us anticipate tomorrow. And let's start with the Internet. Right now, most people on the Internet are connected through a telephone wire and a modem. And while modern personal computers are capable of providing a decent multimedia experience, the phone line and modem trick just don't ring true for much more than text and still images coming over the wire. There is simply too much information that must be transmitted to your computer in order to provide a smooth multimedia experience, and today's phone lines and modems just don't cut it. There must be a faster, more reliable way of getting the information off the network and into your computer. Enter your friendly cable television provider.

Cable Connections

Many cable television companies are currently experimenting with the ability to provide affordable, lightning-fast Internet access over their very own broadcast cables, meaning the same folks who bring you pay-per-view television may soon bring you worldwide network access through the same cable.

▶ *If interactive gambling and games shows were the only types of multimedia coming down the pike for our televisions of the future, living rooms across the nation would be littered with even more couch potatoes! Luckily, exciting edutainment programs, interactive movies, and informative interactive TV broadcasts will lure many would-be spuds away from the temptation of these televised vices.*

Unlike pay-per-view, however, don't expect to pay for individual access to individual pieces of network information. There's simply too much information out there for these folks to keep track of. Instead, expect to pay a single monthly fee for which you'll receive television, satellite, and network access. Rather than tangle yourself up in the cables and wires now par for the on-line course, plug a single cable into the back of your cable-ready computer and away you'll go.

interactive television Telvision of the future, providing viewers with the ability to interact with a broadcast just as they interact with multimedia on personal computers today.

But what if you want to watch TV instead of cruising the Net? Well, you can have a few of these multipurpose cables installed around the house, or better yet, watch your favorite shows directly on your computer. How convenient, no? But don't TV and interactive multimedia really belong in two different categories, to be enjoyed on two different devices? For the time being, yes. But stay tuned. . . .

In many parts of the country *interactive television* is now being tested, allowing home viewers to order movies on demand and participate firsthand in game shows, shopping sprees, and even gamble from the comfort of their living rooms using nothing more than a remote control. Pretty heady stuff, and it's just the beginning. I can see the future, and it's full of couch potatoes gone bad. Luckily, by the time these initial forms of interactive television become widely available, there will be just as many exciting edutainment and multimedia reference programs to tune into through which you can justify your couch-potato tendencies. Yet, regardless of which programs you actually participate in, you'll do it using nothing more than a souped-up remote control pointed at your interactive television.

College Connections

On a slightly brighter note, many colleges are now working with savvy cable companies, wiring campus class rooms, dorms, and labs for television, satellite, and network access using a single cable. Forget hectic freshman orientation. Tomorrow's students will use their trusty remote control to attend televised class meetings and courses. If you're concerned that many students won't bother to tune into required meetings or courses when more interesting shows abound on other stations, don't worry. It's possible to simply broadcast the orientation on all stations or block access to anything but specific televised meetings and courses during the day. It seems that nearly anything is possible. And the best part is that this technology is being used today; it's not lurking somewhere off in the distance.

The Future Is Almost Here

On the horizon twinkles the promise of fully integrated televisions and computers, the seeds of which are now being planted. Many people debate whether the two will actually converge into one device, since they now provide such radically different services, and current efforts to combine the two devices haven't resulted in a successful commercial product.

On the one hand, we have a simple television set that does nothing more than deliver audio and video taken from an antenna or cable. On the other hand, we have a powerful tool capable of providing true interaction with any combination of audio, video, and text. What remains to be seen is how the two will work together, although you can bet televisions of the future will have a substantial amount of computing horsepower beneath the hood regardless of the outcome.

In order to provide effective interactive television that allows us to filter out all the unwanted transmissions, which will inevitably come with 500 or more television stations, computing power is a must. Without computing power, we would be forced to navigate several hundred preprogrammed stations with nothing more than a standard remote control. Toss in a heap of computing power, however, and truly interactive television takes off.

However, the two need not ever converge into a single do-it-all device. We may have a good amount of computing power in our televisions of the future, but never have the need for anything more than a fancy remote control. Even technology buffs question whether the world would really use a combination computer and television. Attempts have been made in the past to market just such a device, such as Apple's MacTV, without success.

Early Attempts

A few years ago Apple Computer introduced a sleek black box designed to provide the best of both worlds, and for a while it seemed like this box had a fighting chance. But it failed as a consumer device, largely because it was neither a great television nor a great computer. It was lukewarm on both fronts, and so people stuck to their tried-and-true televisions and computers.

Keep your eye on these innovative devices as they evolve, however. Even the first microwave ovens were a dismal failure. Most revolutionary products are, since they don't fit into traditional and established markets by their very nature and so are often shunned by consumers.

Where Does Convergence Get Us?

And what if the two do eventually converge into a single device? Say for a moment that the computer and television were one and the same. What does this buy us? Ignoring for a moment the obvious problems of working late into the night while your family screams that you're hogging the "Teleputer," what might a combination of the two provide?

Hollywood in the Digital Age

For one, Hollywood would become fully digital. This is very different from the interactive multimedia movies we have been talking about so far. If television and computers were to actually converge into a single device, you wouldn't need to drop a CD-ROM into your computer to participate in an interactive movie. In this case, you'd simply tune into your television as you normally do. The difference, however, would be that the broadcasts you would tune into would be interactive. You would participate in the action through your television, not through your computer. This is a very important distinction, since we can already get interactive movies on the computer. The television, however, has never been an interactive device. In essence, your television would become more like your computer.

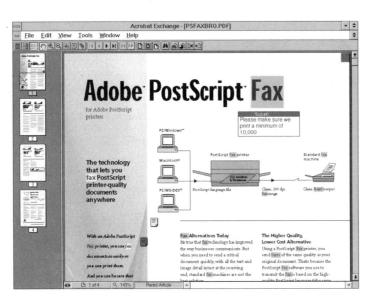

▶ *Adobe* Acrobat *combines many products into one, making it a robust tool for multimedia developers. Using* Acrobat, *you can create hypertext and hypermedia multimedia products with ease. These may be relatively simple products such as company brochures and newsletters, or extremely complex products such as interactive books and reference materials.*

Evolving Television

Most of what you previously enjoyed on television as a passive viewer would eventually become interactive, in various degrees. You might simply experience a movie through the eyes and ears of your favorite character, or you might participate in the event as a full participant. Whatever you did, whatever you said, would become part of the movie. The other characters in the movie, some being real actors, some digital actors, and some home participants such as yourself, would respond accordingly. Your every move, every word would be taken into account and responded to by others in the movie. Given this, you would be able to participate in the same interactive movie any number of times, each time doing and saying what you'd like and so creating a unique experience. Sounds bizarre, but it would be possible. But frankly, my dear, you may not give a damn.

edutainment Educational multimedia products that not only teach but also entertain in the process. Learning with edutainment is a blast since you can have fun while being taught something. The best edutainment products make you forget you are learning.

entertainment Multimedia products designed to be used for pleasure, rather than learning purposes. Arcade, mystery, and adventure games are just a few examples of entertainment products.

Edutainment and Entertainment Down the Road

So what else can we expect in the future? Certainly the way in which we experience education and entertainment will change forever, regardless of what happens on the television front. Entertainment will become something we expect to interact with, even if it's as simple as choosing the camera angle during a movie or pressing a button to watch an instant replay during a televised sporting event. These capabilities already exist.

If television and computers fully converge, we would expect to be in control of any broadcast at any point in time while having the option of participating in the event as well. It may seem like pure fantasy, but then again nearly everything going on in the multimedia world today point toward these possibilities.

At the very least, fully interactive, wholly absorbing movies and multimedia products will eventually arrive on our home computers. These movies and products will be so realistic in sight and sound that they'll make us wonder how we ever managed to enjoy ourselves back in the dark ages of television. In the meantime, today's innovative CD-ROM titles and fast, graphically based Internet access will start us on the path to a future teaming with multimedia promises.

Promises to Keep

It's impossible to know if the promise of every multimedia possibility will be fulfilled. It's likely that some will fall by the wayside as the industry shakes out, if only to be replaced by even more fantastic and unbelievable uses of the technology.

Just as those who witness the dawn of any new age, we can't be sure what lies beyond the horizon. Yes, we can look at the past and project into the future, but what we hope for and expect aren't always what we get.

Whatever the end result, we can be confident that nearly every home computer in the future will be multimedia capable. Today you wouldn't dream of buying a computer incapable of providing word processing at the very least, and in the future you'll expect much, much more from your machine.

Our main senses are those of sight, sound, and touch. It stands to reason that we can expect computers of the future to address these senses with ease, especially since many of today's machines already do. Today you see, hear, and interact with multimedia. Tomorrow you'll see it clearer, hear it better, and interact with it faster. All within a price range you can handle.

Our closing in on the year 2000 marks only the second time that modern man has stepped over the threshold of time and into a new millennium, and it also marks the first time mankind has truly interacted with a machine. Between now and then, there will be scores of software and hardware developers, authoring wizards, artists, sound engineers, interface designers, content developers, and authors working feverishly against the clock to bring about the revolution that has only just begun.

The year 2000 is an imaginary deadline for many in the computer industry, whether self-imposed or real, as we drive towards changing the future through the promise of new technology. Over the next five years an incredible and diverse array of products, services, and concepts will come and go in our quest to step out of the industrial age and into an information age. There is much work to be done if we are to transform our vision of the future from a dream into reality, with miles to go before we sleep and many, oh so many, promises to keep.

APPENDIX A

How to Shop for a Multimedia Computer

Choosing a Platform

The first step in buying a multimedia computer is deciding on which platform is best for you: either an Apple Macintosh- or Microsoft Windows-based system. If you have never used a computer before, or haven't used one much, I suggest the Apple Macintosh platform. The Macintosh is renowned for its ease of installation and use, and it makes a great multimedia computer for first-time owners. If, on the other hand, you want your new computer to double as a work machine so you can bring your work home from the office, chances are you'll need a computer running Microsoft Windows. Although Windows-based computers can be somewhat more difficult to get up and running, if you use one at the office, you'll already be comfortable with this platform.

If you are unclear as to which platform is right for you, don't rush it. Instead, take your time and do a little research. Ask coworkers and friends what they recommend, and why. Take a trip to your local computer superstore and take the demo units for a spin. Be sure to ask the salesperson any questions that come to mind. Sashay on down to your closest magazine stand and browse the various computer publications on display; "Mac or Windows?" is a topic you're likely to find addressed in more than a few articles. Above all else, ask your local user group what it recommends and if it offers any seminars or courses that might help you make a decision. Buying a multimedia computer is a serious investment that will cost around $2,000–$3,000. You can't take too much time making up your mind, and you shouldn't make a final decision without having seriously considered your options.

Configuration Choices

Once you have decided on a platform, you must decide on the specific configuration, that is, the components you want on your system. Just as automobiles come in all shapes and sizes, so too do computers. Similar to Ford or Chevrolet offering dozens of different vehicles in an effort to suit every buyer's needs and desires, computer manufacturers offer a wide choice of computer systems from which to choose. When buying a car, you don't simply walk away from the dealership owning a Ford or Chevy. You walk away the proud owner of a new Bronco, Taurus, or Camaro. If you are in the market for a sports car, you wouldn't consider a station wagon.

The same is true with computers. A multimedia computer is one of the highest performing personal computers you can buy; it is the sports car of computers. Don't make the mistake of assuming that all computers are created equal when it comes to multimedia, or you just might walk away with a station wagon when what you really need is a high-performance sports car. The best way to determine what you're getting in either case, be it a car or computer, is by looking under the hood.

Central Processing Unit (CPU)

The heart of the computer, the Central Processing Unit (CPU), is analogous to the engine of a car: It provides the raw horsepower that drives the entire system. Regardless of what the body of a car looks like, the engine is what counts. The same is true for a computer; the best looking computer on the outside isn't worth a plugged nickel when it comes to multimedia unless a high performance CPU is on the inside. For best all-around performance, go with state of the art CPUs. For Macintosh, this means PowerPC, while Windows systems will use Pentium. Even among these top-of-the-line CPU chips, there are a number of choices, and the savvy consumer will track down the most powerful chip. For most of us, however, simply getting into a multimedia system powered by a PowerPC or Pentium CPU is enough. Even the least powerful versions of each of these CPUs will deliver excellent multimedia.

Although you can get adequate multimedia from computers driven by older, less powerful CPUs, the price difference between these outdated chips and a state-of-the-art PowerPC or Pentium is so narrow that I wouldn't recommend it. Buying into older technology is fine if you simply want to run most of today's multimedia titles, but you may find these systems struggling to keep up with the most demanding titles. And as future multimedia titles become even more demanding in their system requirements, these older CPUs just won't keep pace. However, if you aren't terribly interested in new multimedia software products coming down the pike, a system built around an older CPU may be just right for you. If you do decide to save a few dollars and stick with older technology, be certain that what you buy provides at least enough power to play the majority of today's multimedia titles. Again, you must look under the hood and at the CPU driving the system.

▶ Macintosh CPU—For Macintosh buyers, the very least you'll need is a Motorola 68030 CPU, or better yet, a 68040. These older CPUs are capable of providing decent multimedia and are still plentiful. Don't, however, go any lower than the 68030. Stay far away from the original 68000 and the 68020, which followed closely on its heels. These CPUs don't have anywhere near the power needed to deliver adequate multimedia, and they shouldn't be considered, regardless of how inexpensive the system may be.

▶ Windows-based CPU—In the case of Windows systems, it's a good idea not to go any lower than the Intel 486 CPU. Although a 386 might do the job, you won't get much distance out of a system built around this CPU and will eventually need to upgrade in order to run today's most demanding titles. If you intend to run the majority of products available today and want enough power to drive many of tomorrow's titles as well, get into a 486 system or better. Stay away from 386-based systems if possible, and if you happen upon a 286-based system, turn and run. You'll never get today's multimedia titles running smoothly with a 286-based system and so should never consider buying into this ancient technology.

Although seasoned computer buyers can find excellent deals when it comes to older technology by purchasing used equipment, I wouldn't recommend bargain hunting for first-time buyers. Used computer systems are available through newspaper want ads, user groups, and computer dealers, and can be quite a bargain if you know what to look for. These systems rarely come with a warranty and are more risky to buy than a used car; you never really know what you're getting until it's too late to return it. Stick with new equipment whenever possible, and save yourself unnecessary problems that often accompany used equipment.

Selecting Basic Multimedia Devices

Regardless of the platform you decide on and the CPU you choose to power your system, your system must include the basic multimedia devices: a color monitor, a CD-ROM drive, and multimedia speakers. With Windows-based computers, you must also be sure each device comes with an appropriate adapter board. A video board and sound board are needed with Windows systems, whereas Macintosh systems come with these built in. It isn't enough to ensure that a video and audio board are included; you must be certain that each board is compatible with the device to which it is attached.

Rather than assembling a system piece by piece, it is much easier to purchase a preassembled multimedia computer. Not only do these systems come with compatible devices preinstalled, many come with a number of the best multimedia titles on the market today. These bundles are a great way to get into multimedia effortlessly and often are less expensive than assembling a system from scratch.

Whether you purchase your system piece by piece or as bundle, each component must be up to snuff when it comes to multimedia. Bundles usually are, although you should never buy into one without first verifying its capabilities. At a minimum, your system must have enough high-speed random access memory (RAM) and hard drive space to accommodate a variety of multimedia titles. The monitor must display color, and it must also have a resolution capable of displaying high resolution multimedia images. The CD-ROM drive must be at least double speed, and the speakers must be shielded. If any component in your system is inadequate, it will hold back the entire system and make for a disappointing multimedia experience.

Luckily, clear guidelines are available for you to follow when making your decisions. Tables A-1 and A-2 define the minimum capacities of each multimedia device, allowing you to determine quickly if a system (or device) you are considering is up to snuff. Since all modern computers come standard with a mouse and keyboard (regardless of platform or performance capabilities), these items aren't listed in either table.

Table A-1 describes the minimum requirements needed for both Macintosh and Windows multimedia systems to ensure that you'll get adequate performance from most of today's titles. However, to get the best performance possible, while preparing for tomorrow's demanding multimedia titles, follow the recommended guidelines given in Table A-2.

Table A-1. Minimum Multimedia Configurations

Platform	Macintosh	Windows
Operating System	System 6.0.5 (System 7.0 is required for demanding titles)	DOS 5 (or greater) MS Windows 3.1
CPU	Motorola 68030	Intel 486
RAM	8MB or greater	8MB or greater
Hard Drive	200MB	200MB
CD-ROM Drive	double speed (2x) Hierarchical File System (HFS) capable	double speed (2x) MPC level 2 compliant
	ISO 9600 capable	ISO 9600 capable
	High Sierra capable	CD-ROM X/A capable
	Kodak Photo CD capable	Kodak Photo CD capable
Audio	8-bit digital sound	Sound Blaster compatible
	shielded speakers	16-bit digital sound
		20 synthesizer voices
		MIDI compatible
		shielded speakers
Video	640 x 480 resolution	Super VGA (SVGA)
	8-bit (256 colors) or greater	640 x 480 resolution 8-bit (256 colors) or greater

Table A-2. Recommended Multimedia Configurations

Platform	Macintosh	Windows
Operating System	System 7.1.2 (or greater)	DOS 5 (or greater) MS Windows 3.11 Windows 95
CPU	PowerPC	Intel Pentium
RAM	16MB or greater	16MB or greater
Hard Drive	500MB or greater	500MB or greater
CD-ROM Drive	double speed (2x) or faster	double speed (2x) or faster
	Hierarchical File System (HFS) capable	MPC level 2 compliant
	ISO 9600 capable	ISO 9600 capable
	High Sierra capable	CD-ROM X/A capable
	Kodak Photo CD capable	Kodak Photo CD capable
Audio	16-bit digital sound	Sound Blaster compatible
	shielded speakers	16-bit digital sound
		32 synthesizer voices
		MIDI compatible shielded speakers

(continued)

(continued)

Platform	Macintosh	Windows
Video	640 x 480 resolution or greater 16-bit (65,536 colors) or greater	Super VGA (SVGA) 640 x 480 resolution or greater 16-bit (65,536 colors) or greater

Multimedia Personal Computer (MPC) Specifications

To enable people to easily recognize, purchase, or assemble a multimedia computer system, a group of industry experts developed a set of guidelines known as the MPC (Multimedia Personal Computer) standard. This standard detailed the minimum components required for a multimedia computer powered by the Intel line of CPUs, giving the technical specifications of each component. By adhering to MPC guidelines, you could be sure your Intel computer was multimedia capable. The MPC standard applied only to Intel-based systems; Macintosh computers weren't included.

The original set of MPC specifications was built around the Intel 286 CPU, which you'll recall isn't capable of powering most of today's multimedia titles. As the Intel line of CPUs grew, and multimedia titles began demanding more and more power, the MPC standard was updated. MPC2, as the latest MPC standard is known, specifies a multimedia computer built around the Intel 386 CPU and calls for more random access memory (RAM), hard drive space, and a host of other additions to the original specification. Over time, however, the MPC2 standard has eventually become outdated as well.

Currently, there are no new MPC standards from which you might assemble an adequate multimedia computer today. Although some might contend that the MPC2 standard is still capable of providing a solid multimedia experience, the reality is that these specifications don't address the requirements of today's most demanding multimedia titles and certainly won't give you a system on which you can run tomorrow's titles. MPC is now clearly obsolete, as so many products soon become in this fast-moving industry, with MPC2 close on its heels.

Understanding this, and understanding the need to build multimedia systems today that aren't immediately outdated tomorrow, I have recommended a minimum multimedia system based partly on the MPC2 standard and partly on the requirements of modern multimedia titles. Think of these minimum multimedia requirements as a beefed-up MPC2 specification; any titles capable of running under MPC2 will run perfectly, although somewhat smoother, under this minimum system. In addition, this minimum system will run many demanding titles that MPC2 systems simply cannot, while also providing a configuration under which many of tomorrow's multimedia will also run. In short, I took the best of MPC2 and added the resources you'll need to keep pace with today's, and many of tomorrow's, multimedia products.

Multimedia Upgrade Kits

If you already own a computer that meets the minimum CPU requirements listed in Table A-1, you may find it more cost effective to simply purchase an upgrade kit rather than buy a complete multimedia system. In this case, each component in the upgrade kit must be at or above the minimum configuration specifications listed.

In addition, each component in the upgrade kit must be compatible with your system. The easiest way to check compatibility is to ask the salesperson. Of course, this assumes that you know the make and configuration of your current system, so you may have to dig through the documentation that came with your computer.

You may also find that your older personal computer operating system is not up to speed. For a Macintosh, you'll need to have at least System 6.0.5 installed, although System 7.0 (or greater) is required by many of the most demanding multimedia titles. Non-Macintosh computers should be upgraded to Windows 3.11, which may require an upgrade to the basic Disk Operating System (DOS) as well.

If your system isn't currently running the minimum operating system, there is a good chance you'll first need to install more random access memory (RAM) in order to upgrade. Many older systems have just enough RAM to get by, so you must ensure that at least 4MB is installed before proceeding with the upgrade, although I recommend 8MB of RAM or more for any multimedia system. Installing RAM is a tricky business, best left to the professionals. The same is true for hard drives. Although your older system may have been just fine with a small hard drive, a decent multimedia system should have at least 200MB of space. It's possible to squeeze by with as little as 80MB of hard drive space when you first begin to use multimedia, but you'll need to upgrade as you begin to use more than a handful of multimedia titles.

Before buying a multimedia upgrade kit, you should calculate the final price of getting your current system up to speed. Multimedia upgrade kits are ideal for some computers, but the cost of getting many older systems up to speed isn't worth the effort. By the time you've upgraded your current system's RAM, hard drive, operating system, and also purchased and installed a multimedia upgrade kit, it may be that you could have saved time and perhaps even money by simply buying a new multimedia computer altogether.

Getting On-Line: Modem Requirements

If you're itching to get into the on-line action, you'll need to add one last piece of equipment to your multimedia system: a modem. Similar to every other component in your multimedia system, the modem must be powerful enough to deliver a decent on-line experience.

The measure of a modem's power is in raw speed, often referred to as *baud rate* or *bits per second* (bps for short). Although baud rate and bps are not exactly the same thing, the terms are very close in meaning and are often used interchangeably. These two terms provide a measurement of how fast a modem can send and receive information. The higher the baud rate or bps, the faster the modem. It all boils down to speed: the faster the modem, the better your on-line experience.

Many modems also feature fax-send and fax-receive capabilities. With these capabilities, you not only have access to the on-line world, but you'll also have what amounts to a full-blown facsimile machine on your computer. Not all modems feature fax send and fax receive, however. If these features are important to you, ensure the modem you buy provides fax capabilities. If you are only concerned with getting on-line, fax capabilities may be of no interest to you at all.

Modems come in two forms: internal and external. Although internal modems are hidden away out of view and can make for a less-tangled computer setup, they are also more difficult to install. I favor external modems since they are simple to install and can be upgraded easily. Regardless of which type you choose, the modem must be both fast enough to provide adequate on-line access and compatible with existing on-line services and fax machines.

The minimum speed for decent on-line access is 9600 bps, although I recommend 14,400 bps. A 9600 bps modem will get you on-line and give you access to the networked world, but you'll spend a good deal of time waiting for graphics and files to transfer to your computer. Buying a 14,400 bps modem (14.4 Kbps, for short) will give you much faster access to the on-line world and decrease the amount of time you spend waiting for items to transfer to and from your computer. Most on-line services charge by the minute, meaning you pay for every minute you are connected. As a result, you'll spend less money on phone bills (modems transfer information using telephone lines) and on-line service fees if you get a faster modem.

Think of a slow modem as a gas-guzzling car: You'll get where you want to go eventually, but it will take longer than you expected and cost twice as much in fuel. For this very reason you might consider buying a 28,800 bps modem (28.8 Kbps). These speed demons are the fastest modems you can buy at the moment and will give you a smooth on-line experience, while also lowering your telephone bills and on-line service fees. Many commercial on-line services don't currently provide 28.8 Kbps access, but most are now testing these high speed connections. Expect leading on-line services such as America Online, CompuServe, and Prodigy to provide 28.8 Kbps access by the end of 1995.

Modems can be very tricky to configure properly, so you should expect to spend some time tweaking the settings of your new unit while on the phone with technical support. This is a fact of modem life, since there are so many different types of modems floating around in the world today. To make dealing with a modem easier, you should purchase one that is "Hayes Compatible." Hayes is a leader among modem manufacturers and has practically set the standard to which other modems are compared. As such, any modem you buy that is compatible with Hayes will likely be much easier to get up and running smoothly with on-line services.

CCITT Specifications

Your modem should also conform to a set of specifications established by the International Telegraph and Telephone Consultative Committee (CCITT). CCITT was formed to develop international standards for data and facsimile transmission speeds. The standards established by CCITT correspond directly to bps, and often begin with "V." followed by a number (V.32, for example). Table A-3 gives the most commonly used CCITT specifications, together with corresponding bps speeds.

Table A-3. Key to CCITT Specifications

CCITT Specification	Bits Per Second (bps)
V.22	1200 modem
V.22bis	2400 modem
V.27ter	4800 fax
V.29	9600 fax
V.32	9600 modem
V.32bis	14,400 modem
V.17	14,400 fax
V.34	28,800 modem

If you buy a modem that conforms to CCITT standards and is Hayes compatible, you'll avoid a great deal of hassle when configuring your modem for on-line access. For instance, if you were in the market for a 14,400 bps modem, your best bet would be one advertised as "14.4 Kbps, V.32bis Hayes Compatible." This modem would be about as standard and universally accepted as you could hope to find, and it wouldn't require much effort to configure it properly.

The Bottom Line

Whether you are buying a new multimedia computer, upgrading your existing system, or simply buying a modem in order to jump into the on-line action, the most important aspects of any purchase you make are the technical support, manufacturer's warranty, and satisfaction guarantee terms that accompany your purchase.

The multimedia computer industry is a fast and competitive one, with manufacturers and resellers popping up just about everywhere you look today. They are vying for your business and are willing to make investing in their goods as convenient and worry-free as possible. Products that don't come with solid technical support, a reasonable product warranty, and even some type of satisfaction guarantee aren't worth spending your money on. You want the best equipment your money can buy, and the deal must include technical support, a product warranty, and a guarantee that you will actually get what you are paying for.

Technical Support

At the very least, your new equipment should come with 30 days of free technical support. Some vendors offer lifelong technical support, which means you can call for help as long as you own the equipment. Lifelong support is quite a deal and is worth looking for when you're shopping around. A year of technical support is more common, although the terms vary from vendor to vendor. Never, however, buy into equipment with less than 30 days of free technical support. Although you'll run into most of your problems during the first month of use, you are practically guaranteed to run into other problems later on. The vast majority of problems you will encounter can be resolved easily by placing a phone call to technical support, and if the support isn't available, you'll be stranded.

Manufacturer's Warranty

The product warranty specifies the terms and duration surrounding the manufacturer's obligation to replace or fix your equipment in the event of failure. Although some manufacturers do provide lifelong warranties, one year is more common. Some warranty periods are as little as 90 days, and I wouldn't consider buying products offering less. If the manufacturer doesn't believe its equipment is worth at least a 90 day warranty, it probably isn't worth buying to begin with.

Satisfaction Guaranteed

Although products come with technical support and a manufacturer's warranty, the product reseller usually provides the satisfaction guarantee. With a satisfaction guarantee you are free to use the product for a specific amount of time and may return it for a full refund or store credit if you aren't satisfied with it. This is quite a deal, which not all resellers offer, although many computer superstores do. I recently purchased an entire multimedia system from a local superstore, and now have 30 days to decide if it is right for me. If I don't like it, for whatever reason, I can return it within a month for a full refund. Now that's a deal I couldn't pass up, and I would recommend buying your equipment under similar terms whenever possible.

APPENDIX B

How to Shop for Multimedia Software

Look Before You Leap

Shopping for titles may sound like the easiest part of getting into multimedia, but it isn't. If you are tempted to walk into a computer superstore and cruise the aisles while tossing the most exciting-looking titles into your shopping cart, STOP! This technique is akin to shopping for groceries on an empty stomach: everything you see looks scrumptious, but you'll end up with an awful lot more than you really need, and you will have spent far too much in the process. A better approach is the one suggested in Appendix A for buying a multimedia computer. Take your time, know what to look for, know what to look out for, shop around, and find the best deal you can.

The first step involves knowing what products will run on your multimedia computer. Although some multimedia CD-ROMs can run on both Macintosh- and Windows-based machines, this is not usually the case. Cross platform products such as these are certainly convenient, especially if you use both Macintosh- and Windows-based computers. However, most titles come on platform-specific CD-ROMs, so it is very important that you only buy titles that will run on your computer.

Luckily, good product packaging makes this process quite simple. On the box of any multimedia product you will find a listing of system requirements, or specifications. A product's system requirements detail the platform and minimum configuration necessary to use that title. A set of recommended specifications often is provided, listing the optimal equipment and configuration needed to get the best performance out of a title. To see if a product will run on your machine, simply look on the packaging for the system requirements. And if you buy a product over the phone, for example, through a mail order company, ask the salesperson to tell you the system requirements. If your system provides the minimum requirements needed by a title, it should run fine when you get it home. Fine, that is, if no special requirements are listed.

Special Requirements

In addition to providing the specifications required for use, many titles also list special requirements. For example, you might need extra RAM, beyond what most programs require. More often than not, however, special requirements refer to software or hardware that must be in place before you can use the title.

Special Multimedia Software

Typically, special requirements for a product will include specialized software that makes it possible for your computer to play motion video. Although your multimedia computer is already capable of playing motion video in terms of its raw horsepower, the software required to make it all happen must also be in place. Most new multimedia computers come with this software preinstalled, although some do not. Luckily, the vast majority of titles that require motion video software also happen to provide it, for just such occasions. Simply install it, and you're up and running.

QuickTime

Multimedia products for Apple Macintosh computers often require QuickTime, which is the software that allows the Macintosh to play motion video. It also provides a host of standard multimedia functions such as audio and video compression, audio and video decompression, and synchronization of audio and video sources. QuickTime is a vital part of any Macintosh multimedia system and comes standard on all new Macintosh computers. If you attempt to run a title that requires QuickTime, and it is not installed, the software will fail to work properly and will, in most cases, tell you why. In this case, simply dig out the operating system disks that came with your Macintosh and look for the one labeled QuickTime. Insert the disk into your computer and open the Read Me file, which explains how to install QuickTime. This is a fast and painless process, and you'll have QuickTime up and running in no time.

QuickTime for Windows

Although it is considered primarily a Macintosh product, QuickTime is also available for Windows-based computers. When a multimedia product specifies QuickTime for Windows, you'll probably need to install it yourself because few Windows-based computers come with QuickTime preinstalled. If this is the case, check the product to see if it provides the QuickTime software. Chances are it does, but if it doesn't, check the set of disks that came with your computer. If it isn't there either, contact your local computer superstore, user group, or mail order company, and ask specifically for QuickTime for Windows. Once you have it in hand, the process of installing QuickTime on a Windows computer is just as easy as on the Macintosh. Just pop in the installation disk, follow the installation instructions, and QuickTime for Windows will be up and running in no time flat.

Video for Windows

Although QuickTime is often required by Windows multimedia products, you're more likely to find Video For Windows (VFW) listed among the special requirements. VFW is very similar to QuickTime, providing the software required for many multimedia functions on the Windows platform. Many Windows titles that require VFW will provide it in case your computer doesn't already have it installed. Just as with QuickTime, if VFW isn't already installed, you must locate the installation disks that contain this special software and update your computer. Look first throughout the set of disks that came with your computer, and if you don't find it, contact your local computer superstore, user group, or a mail order company.

Special Hardware Requirements

The most demanding multimedia products often require specialized hardware. Typically, the special hardware needed is nothing more than a fast CPU, usually the Motorola 68030 or the Intel 486. If your system configuration complies with the minimum setup listed in Appendix A, you won't have a problem. In this case you already have enough horsepower to run the overwhelming majority of multimedia products requiring a fast CPU.

Sometimes, however, special hardware requirements may include high performance video or audio boards. Again, if you follow the minimum configuration requirements found in Appendix A, your machine should play the majority of these titles as well.

Specialized MPEG hardware

Although it is very rare, highly specialized multimedia products, such as those found in the medical and scientific industry, may require highly specialized boards dedicated to compressing and decompressing audio and/or video sources. The most popular of these boards utilize a compression/decompression technique known as MPEG, which provides incredibly fast full-motion video. Dedicated MPEG boards produce extremely smooth and fast full-motion video, of considerably higher quality than that typically found with QuickTime or VFW. Most consumer-oriented titles do not require this level of performance, however, and do just fine using motion video software.

Leap, But Leap with Caution

After you've made sure a title of interest is compatible with your multimedia system, the question then becomes "Should I buy it?" Again, as with any other purchase related to multimedia, I tend to play it safe and err on the side of caution. There are simply too many titles floating around out there to merely pick one off the shelf and walk up to the checkout counter with it. Remember, the packaging is the best part of many multimedia products that seem fantastic on the outside, yet are without substance on the inside. Why risk it and waste your money?

Friends, Coworkers, and Relatives

The best way to choose a product is through the recommendation of someone you trust. This could be a friend, coworker, or relative. People you know and trust, who have actually had their hands on a product, are the best sources of unbiased opinion you can find. If they like it, chances are you'll like it. And if they don't, what are the chances you will?

Product Reviewers

My favorite source of recommendations are product reviews in industry journals and magazines. Just about all of these publications feature regular multimedia reviews, and many also list the reviewer's favorite titles in each major category (reference, entertainment, edutainment, and so on), complete with detailed descriptions of each title. Product reviewers are often the most conservative when it comes to recommending products. They must filter through hundreds of titles each month, and only the best of the bunch will make it to print. When a product reviewer gives a title high marks, you can bet it is a worthwhile product. And when these professional software users recommend that you stay away from particular products, their advice is worth listening to.

User Groups

User groups are also an excellent source of multimedia product recommendations. Many user groups publish their own lists of favorite products and often recommend which ones to steer clear of. In addition, many user groups provide a place where you can test drive current titles, further ensuring you know what you're getting before you pay for a particular product.

Everyone Has an Opinion

However you go about it, get an opinion on multimedia products before you put down cash, check, or credit card. There are literally thousands of multimedia titles on the market today, with new products hitting the shelves so fast it is almost impossible to keep up. Although many of these are excellent products worth buying, many are not. Save yourself both hassle and money, and get the opinion of someone who has used the product. Finding someone who has an opinion about a product you're interested in won't be very difficult. Everyone has an opinion, and the multimedia industry is no exception.

Safety Net

Regardless of which products you decide to buy, it is critical you have a safety net in case you come across a product that fails to meet your expectations. Sometimes you'll find that a multimedia product simply doesn't work for you, that it fails to meet your expectations despite the number of people who rave about it. And as with any consumer product, you should have a safety net: the right to return it.

Before buying any product, ask the seller about its return policy. Although very few offer a money-back guarantee on software products, most will extend a store credit good toward the purchase of another product. If you happen upon a vendor that fails to provide a return policy, turn around and walk out (or hang up the phone). With very little effort you will find a reputable vendor that offers a return policy, whether through store credit or a refund.

Best Bang for Your Buck

Once you start shopping around for multimedia titles, you'll begin to see the stiff competition in this booming industry. There are scores of multimedia software companies out there, all vying for your business. In order to reach customers in such a competitive market, many of these companies offer products at drastically reduced prices just to get their foot in the door. Their reasoning: If you like what you've bought at a reduced price, you'll be likely to purchase upgrades to that product or even other products they offer. These low cost "loss-leader" products, as they are called, are plentiful and can be rooted out with a little effort on your part.

Promotions

The first place you'll find deals on multimedia products is your computer superstore or mail order catalog. Walk in (or call, as the case may be) and ask the first salesperson you make contact with if there are any promotions going on. Most of these places have several promotional deals going at once, and you're likely to find top-notch products at incredibly low prices. I call a few mail order companies every week or two, just to see what new promotions they have. In fact, the month this book went to print I bought the complete works of Shakespeare on CD-ROM and a fabulous multimedia encyclopedia for only $12.95 each. I snapped up both of these products for about half the price I would have paid for only one of them anywhere else, all thanks to a little phone work.

Software Bundles

Another great way to get fantastic deals on products is through software bundles, which are really glorified loss-leader promotions, but on a larger scale. By selling many promotional multimedia products together as a bundle, vendors can give you several products at a fraction of what they would cost individually. Again, the rationale is that if you like what you see, you'll upgrade or buy other products at the full price later.

Some bundles are assembled by the reseller, such as computer stores and mail order companies. In this case, the reseller groups several promotional titles together and sells the whole bunch as an affordable bundle. Other bundles are created by multimedia software companies. These bundles contain several of the company's products and are offered to the public at a reduced price (either directly or through a reseller). Either way, software bundles are an excellent way to save a bundle of cash on multimedia products.

User Groups

User groups often have the best deals on multimedia products you can find. Since software companies recognize the value of making their products available at a discount to user groups, these organizations frequently offer deals that others can't match. The thinking here is similar to other promotional efforts: Get the products to people at a price they can afford, and they will buy upgrades and other products later on. The key with user groups, however, is in their ability to create great demand for a product simply by word of mouth. A few well-publicized words of praise from top-notch user groups can do wonders for a product fighting for market share, and software companies are fast to realize that the best way to get good user group publicity is to get their products into the hands of these folks fast and cheap.

Rock-bottom Pricing

Although not every title you'll want will be available at a rock-bottom promotional price, it's worth hunting around before springing for the full price. At the very least you'll find the best price around, having compared prices from various sources while looking for these loss-leader bargains. If there is one lesson to be learned about multimedia software, it's this: You'll never pay full price if you simply shop around.

Gotchas

Promotional deals and software bundles can give you the best bang for your buck, but if you don't look carefully at what you're buying, you may not save money at all. Although many promotional deals and software bundles give you the full product, some only give you demonstration versions and limited editions of what you want.

To ensure you're getting the real McCoy, ask the salesperson if the product(s) you are buying are limited in any way. Also, be sure to ask if you are getting the "full commercial version," because you don't want anything less. Limited edition and demonstration versions of a product are something you should get for free. Never pay more than the price of shipping and handling for these watered-down versions of the real thing. Better yet, look a little harder for a full commercial version of the product you want, but at a loss-leader price. Chances are, you will find it.

Reputation, Reputation, Reputation

In an industry overflowing with software companies and products, it's hard to know where to turn. I always opt for products that have a good reputation among users, ideally those created by a reputable software company and sold by an upstanding reseller.

There are, of course, fantastic products and companies just emerging onto the scene, which understandably have no reputation to speak of quite yet. In time, however, excellent companies with excellent products will develop excellent reputations. And your friends, neighbors, coworkers, product reviewers, and user groups will point you toward them. For now, stick with the tried and true.

Tried and True

A few companies that have consistently produced top-notch products are listed in Table B-1. This isn't an all-inclusive list, of course, but will provide you with a solid base from which to begin assembling a library of quality multimedia products. Not every single product produced by these folks is outstanding, but you can be pretty sure they are above average. And when you get your hands on their best stuff, stand back — clear the weekend schedule, unplug the telephone, and brew a fresh pot of coffee: You're in for a superb experience.

Table B-1. Multimedia Library Starter List

Multimedia Software Company	Product Focus
ADAM Technology	reference, edutainment
Brøderbund	edutainment, entertainment
Creative Multimedia	reference, edutainment, entertainment
Interplay	edutainment, music, entertainment
Macromedia	multimedia authoring tools
MECC	edutainment
Microsoft	all categories
Origin Systems, Inc.	entertainment
Virgin Interactive	entertainment
Voyager	educational, edutainment

GLOSSARY

In addition to knowing the various types of multimedia products available, it is also helpful to know the basic jargon used in the industry. Not only will this help you avoid multimedia titles that cannot be used on your computer system, it will also help you better understand what is inside the fancy packaging before you lay down cold, hard cash. Multimedia packaging can often be daunting, if not downright intimidating. Knowing the buzzwords used to advertise multimedia products will alleviate much of the confusion.

3-D Objects or scenes that look as if they are realistic, having depth in addition to height and width. Using sophisticated drawing techniques, computers can create the illusion of depth by shading computerized objects in a manner consistent with real-life objects.

Apple Macintosh operating system The graphically oriented operating system used with Apple Macintosh computers.

artists Creators of artwork needed for multimedia titles. Some create backgrounds, some characters, while others design entire scenes.

Atari A popular home entertainment system.

audio card (sound card) The equipment that makes it possible for computerized sound to be played on speakers. Both an audio card and speakers are required for sound to be heard.

authoring tools Software programs used to create multimedia products.

author An individual who writes scripts, which form the core piece of content from which other content is developed. The author invents and develops the plot, characters, and storyline.

browser Specialized computer software that allows users to visually navigate the contents of the Internet by using a mouse.

bug A problem that prevents a software program from working properly or as expected.

bulletin board system (BBS) A program that lets you use your personal computer to meet and correspond with others (for example, user group members) from the comfort of your home. You can also transfer files and send and receive messages through a BBS.

bundles Two or more products sold together, rather than individually, usually at a price lower than what you would pay if you purchased each product separately. Software bundles are a group of software products gathered together and sold as a single product. Hardware bundles are also common, typically bundled with a number of software products to make the deal more attractive.

CD-ROM (Compact Disc Read Only Memory) A close relative to the audio compact disc we are familiar with. CD-ROMs are able to store many types of media that may be accessed via computer. Because they are small and a massive amount of information may be stored on each disc, CD-ROM has become the most popular way of delivering multimedia to computer users.

CD-ROM drive A device that gives your computer access to the information found on CD-ROMs.

central processing unit (CPU) A computer's CPU is the equivalent of a car's engine. It provides the raw power on which all other parts rely.

clone A computer that looks and acts like a brand name system, yet is not manufactured by the same company. You can often get the same or better performance from a clone than you would with a brand name system, and you'll often save a few dollars in the process.

commercial on-line service Specialized on-line services provided by commercial companies such as America Online, Prodigy, and CompuServe. Commercial on-line services typically provide members with access to a multitude of software products, on-line discussion forums, technical support from a variety of vendors, and the capability to communicate using electronic mail (e-mail).

Commuter TV Specially equipped television sets found in many subway stations across the nation that display general information such as the current time and temperature, in addition to advertisements.

compression Special techniques used to crunch sound and image information down in size. Compression is often applied to images and audio sources that must fit together on a CD-ROM.

content The various components of a multimedia production, such as video, sound, photographs, and text. Content also encompasses nontangible items such as plot and storylines.

content developers Individuals responsible for assembling the various pieces of content that form the basis of any multimedia product.

cross platform compatible Products that allow your work to move smoothly between Macintosh- and Windows-based platforms.

cyberspace A buzzword often used to describe the Internet or any of the commercial services available to consumers seeking access to the Net.

data glove A highly specialized piece of computer equipment that looks like a normal glove, yet when worn transmits hand movements into the computer.

data transfer rate A measure of how fast a CD-ROM drive can get information from the surface of a CD-ROM to you.

decompression Techniques used to re-expand CD-ROM data for playback.

demo version A demonstration version of a software product. Demo versions are often nothing more than multimedia presentations that give you a rough idea of a particular product, although sometimes a demo is an actual product that can be used in a very limited capacity (see limited edition).

digitized Something that has been converted to the computer format, such as artwork or sound.

Disk Operating System (DOS) A text-oriented operating system developed by Microsoft that provided the groundwork for their mouse-driven, graphical operating system, Microsoft Windows.

double-speed (2x) CD-ROM drive Today's standard in CD ROM drives, which is twice as fast as the single-speed drive.

DreamWorks SDK A Hollywood studio founded by entertainment industry gurus Steven Spielberg, Jeffrey Katzenberg, and David Geffen.

edutainment Educational multimedia products that not only teach but also entertain in the process.

entertainment Multimedia products designed to be used for pleasure, rather than learning purposes.

full motion Also referred to as real time or simply motion, full motion describes the quality of playback for a computerized movie or scene. A full-motion movie will play smoothly, without skipping frames or jumping and jerking about.

full screen Images and video residing on computers can be viewed in a variety of sizes, and larger sizes require more computing power. Full screen refers to an image or video that is as large as the monitor, and significant computing power is required for smooth playback.

full version The complete, commercially available version of a software product. The full version of a product is not limited in any way and is what you would expect if you were to purchase the product at the full price.

game port Standard feature on an audio board, allowing you to connect a joystick or other video game controller to your computer.

graphical operating system An operating system that relies heavily on graphic images and the use of a mouse to operate a computer.

graphical user interface (GUI) The visual portion of a graphical operating system, such as windows, icons, menus, and the mouse pointer.

groupware Specialized software that allows people on different computers to share electronic documents, images, voice, and even video.

hacker Counterculture heroes who develop software products and occasionally break into sensitive information systems for the shear joy of discovery.

hard drive A device used to permanently store the operating system and various files needed for multimedia and other programs.

home entertainment systems Small, relatively inexpensive devices that attach to a television and provide entertainment primarily in the form of video games. Extremely popular among teenagers, Atari, Nintendo, and Sega are the most common home entertainment systems in use today.

hypermedia A system that uses the same principles found with hypertext. Photographs, video, sound, and text can be linked to one another to form a system of interconnected media.

hypertext A system that links words and phrases together so you can navigate textual information in a free-form fashion that is faster and more accurate than other methods of searching for information.

information kiosks Informational multimedia products, packaged inside industrial-strength plastic containers approximately 5 feet high by 3 feet wide, that feature touch-sensitive video displays to present and allow interaction with their contents.

information superhighway An analogy often used to describe the Internet.

interactive The ability to navigate the contents of a multimedia product, giving you some degree of control over it.

interactive movies Full-motion, full-color movies we can truly be part of. Delivered on CD-ROM or over the Internet, the interactive multimedia movie requires state-of-the-art hardware and software to be truly realistic.

interactive television Telvision of the future, providing viewers with the ability to interact with a broadcast just as they interact with multimedia on personal computers today.

interface adapter board A board, or card, located inside the computer that is used to connect external devices such as the monitor, CD-ROM drive, and speakers.

interface designer Individuals responsible for designing what you see and use to control or navigate the contents of a multimedia software title.

the Internet A vast, globally connected computer network developed by the United States government after World War II. Although originally designed to provide scientists and researchers with the ability to communicate using computers, the Internet has grown rapidly over the past decade to include a diverse group of approximately 30 million users world-wide.

keyword A word used to search for information when navigating a reference or informational product.

kiosk concierge Information kiosks typically located in hotel lobbies and dedicated to providing information normally available through the hotel concierge.

limited edition A scaled-down version of a software product, often lacking in features or content in order to persuade the customer to purchase the full version.

line in connector Sound board feature that allows you to connect to the board a number of devices, such as an audio CD player, your home stereo, or even the audio portion of a video cassette player.

line out connector Sound board feature that allows you to play computer sounds on devices located outside your computer. For example, you can connect to your computer a set of headphones, speakers, or any other device that would allow you to hear sound.

magnetic shielding Proper covering of the magnets inside the speakers to ensure they do no damage to computer devices.

microphone input port Standard feature on an audio board, allowing you to record sound from your own digital audio sources directly into your computer.

Microsoft Video for Windows Also known as Audio Video Interleaved (AVI), Microsoft Video for Windows is similar in nature to Apple's QuickTime. Full-motion video capabilities are provided without the need for specialized hardware using this technology. Audio is interleaved with video to provide smooth, synchronized playback of both media.

Microsoft Windows operating system A graphically oriented computer operating system developed by Microsoft Corporation.

MIDI (Musical Instrument Digital Interface) MIDI is a specialized music technology, typically a combination of specialized hardware and software, that provides the ability to record and/or play back musical instruments using the computer.

modem A piece of hardware for connecting computers over telephone lines. he most common modems cost around $100, although faster modems can cost more than $300.

monitor (video display) The monitor, or video display, is the part of a computer system that looks like a television screen and allows you to see what is going on inside.

morph Made popular by Michael Jackson and Peter Gabriel music videos, morphing is an extremely popular special effect that permits any object to transform into another object.

mouse A small plastic device attached to the computer by a thin cable through which it communicates with the operating system. Movements of the mouse are translated into movements of a pointer on the computer screen, which in turn is used to navigate the computer.

MPC (Multimedia Personal Computer) A standard in the computer industry, defining the equipment necessary for an Intel-based computer system to be considered multimedia capable.

multimedia A computer product composed of two or more media (sound, video, photography, animation, text, and so on) with which the user can interact.

multimedia presentation A multimedia work you watch but do not participate in.

multimedia product Something you can purchase or otherwise obtain for the express purpose of using in a multimedia capacity.

the Net Shorthand term used interchangeably with "the Internet."

network A system of computers connected to each other for the purpose of data transfer and communications.

Nintendo A popular home entertainment system.

on-board video cards Some computers come with a built-in, or on-board, video card as part of the system. If a computer does not come with a video card, one must be installed before the system can be used.

on-line A buzzword used to describe any activity taking place on a computer network. Although on-line refers to activity taking place on any computer network, those most commonly used today are the Internet, World Wide Web, and/or commercial on-line services, such as America Online, Prodigy, or CompuServe.

operating system The software that makes it possible to use a computer. The operating system is your interface for working with the various components of a computer, such as disk drives, monitors, hard disks, and filing systems.

Pentium A vibrant and powerful new line of Intel CPUs that outperform any previous CPU developed by Intel.

PowerPC An extremely powerful line of CPUs developed by a joint effort between Apple, IBM, and Motorola.

producers Individuals who manage all aspects of multimedia projects, including overseeing actors, artists, sound crews, technology wizards, script writers, and lawyers involved in the projects.

proprietary Any item that is designed to be used only by those who have express permission from the manufacturer.

quad-speed (4x) CD-ROM drive The undisputed champ of CD-ROM drives is, at least for the moment, quadruple-speed (quad-speed or 4x). Quad-speed drives perform four times as fast as their original single-speed ancestors and give the best all-around performance out of the bunch.

QuickTime Developed by Apple Computer, QuickTime is a software product that provides the capability to access sound, video, and animation via computer.

random access memory (RAM) RAM is the high-speed memory, or storage, essential for fast interaction with the computer and software products.

real time You may find, while navigating a multimedia program, that events are a bit sluggish. It may take a few moments for you to go from one place to another, or the glass may take longer than expected to hit the ground when dropped. Many multimedia producers are aware of this disparity between computer and real life. They attempt to provide as realistic an environment as possible by ensuring events in the computer world happen in real time. For the most part, real time means there are no unnatural delays when navigating a multimedia product.

render The use of a computer system in drawing an object or scene that would otherwise require human effort. The initial object or scene is typically sketched by a human while the most difficult portions of the drawing are done by the computer, such as adding color, depth, perspective, shading, and so on.

re-sampling A process in which a sound engineer removes portions of the digial audio information until the sound has been whittled down to a more manageable size.

resolution Technically speaking, resolution is defined by the number of picture elements, or pixels, available for display. Resolution is generally spoken of in terms of width and height, such as 640 x 480 (640 pixels wide by 480 pixels high). The more pixels, the higher the resolution of a device or image.

sampling The process of recording a digital sound.

sample rate A measure of how much audio information is gathered during the sampling process. The higher the sample rate, the higher the quality of sound when played back.

SCSI interface The interface adapter board that comes installed on Apple Macintosh computers, also an option on Windows-based computers.

Sega A popular home entertainment system.

sound card (audio card) The equipment that makes it possible for computerized sound to be played on speakers. Both a sound card and speakers are required for audio to be heard.

sound engineer People involved with sound in multimedia apply skills found in the traditional sound industry (such as recording and editing, dubbing, or generating audio effects, to name a few) to the highly technical field of computerized sound.

speed The speed of a CD-ROM drive is a measure of how fast it can get information from the surface of a CD-ROM to you, also known as the *data transfer rate.*

synchronization Ensuring that audio and video play in sync with each other; for example, making the lips move in time with the voice.

synthesizer The part of a sound board that creates music and sound effects.

synthesizer voices The different voices a synthesizer can produce. An important measure of a synthesizer's quality is the number of voices it can produce.

technology wizards Hardware and software gurus who make it possible to combine audio and visual content with computer interactivity.

texture mapping/surface mapping The ability to take a flat surface, or texture, and wrap it around a 3-D computer object. This technique greatly enhances the realism of an object, which would otherwise be viewed in a solid color or with greatly reduced surface detail.

upgrade kits Multimedia hardware bundles that feature the necessary equipment to make an existing computer system multimedia-capable. These upgrade kits typically include a sound card and speakers, CD-ROM drive, and a number of multimedia titles.

upgrading Replacing or augmenting computer system components to allow the system to run multimedia titles effecively.

user Any person who uses a computer. Many of today's computer users are getting into multimedia to get the most out of their computer systems.

user group A small, privately run computer support organization devoted to the study of, and sharing of information related to, software and/or hardware.

version history A detailed listing that describes the various updates and fixes made on a software product from version to version.

video card The equipment that makes it possible for a video display to work properly. If a computer does not come with a video card, one must be installed before the system can be used.

video conferencing Conferences with a number of people at different locations. Your image and voice are broadcast to all members participating in the conference, while you in turn can see and hear everyone else.

video display (monitor) The video display, or monitor, is the part of a computer system that looks like a television screen and allows you to see what isgoing on inside. Without a monitor, you wouldn't be able to use your computer or see any portion of a multimedia product.

video goggles A highly specialized piece of computer equipment that looks similar to ski goggles (or in some cases, a streamlined motorcycle helmet), yet transmits head movements into the computer and video images to the eyes of the user.

virtual Used to describe anything that isn't real but is simulated so well it almost looks realistic.

virtual reality The ability to move about and control a multimedia experience from your own perspective and as a full participant rather than a passive viewer.

wave-table synthesizer Synthesizers that play digital recordings of sounds, producing better quality audio than FM synthesizers.

World Wide Web A subset of the Internet that has been specially designed for visual access. Given its graphical nature, the World Wide Web is visually navigated using special software known as a browser and easily lends itself to multimedia content.

INDEX

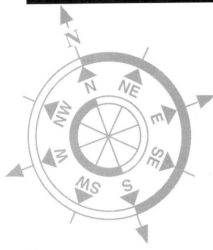

A

actors, 141–142
  See also multimedia people
Adobe
  Acrobat, 44, 172, 202
  Photoshop, 133, 151, 171
advertising
  multimedia, 33–35
  profit and, 35
  See also commercials
Altair computer, 89–90
America Online, 41, 58, 85, 177, 178, 190
  modem speed and, 218
  See also on-line services
Apple Computer
  black box, 201
  history of, 85–86
Apple Macintosh, 85–89, 207
  computer, 87
  CPUs, 88
  graphical interface, 86
  history of, 85–86
  minimum configurations, 212
  mouse, 86
  operating system, 87, 233
  PowerPC, 88–89, 209, 238
  QuickTime and, 224–225, 238
  recommended configurations, 213–214
  SCSI interface, 114, 239
  upgrade kits, 119
  Windows vs., 83–85
  See also operating systems
architecture, 60

artists, 131–133, 151–152
  artwork conversion specialists, 132
  computer, 132–133
  conventional vs. multimedia, 132–133
  defined, 131, 151, 233
  as multimedia career, 151–152
  types of, 132, 151–152
  See also multimedia people
Atari, 16, 51, 56, 66
  defined, 233
  See also home entertainment systems
audio cards, 74–76
  CD–ROM drive compatibility, 115
  defined, 74, 233, 239
  digital audio playback and recording, 116
  function of, 74
  game port, 117, 235
  line in/line out, 116–117
  microphone input port, 117, 237
  MIDI, 75, 116, 195, 237
  minimum requirements, 94
  resolution, 74–75
  standard features, 117
  synthesizer, 115
  synthesizer voices, 116, 239
  in upgrade kits, 115–117
  wave-table synthesizer, 115, 116
  See also multimedia computers; speakers
Audio Video Interleaved (AVI), 237
authoring tools, 138–139, 153
  defined, 233
  See also authors
authoring wizards, 153–154
  defined, 153
  skills of, 153
authors, 140–141, 157–158
  defined, 140, 157, 233
  in group effort, 158
  multimedia careers, 157–158
  multiple, 141
  scripts and, 140, 141, 157
  See also multimedia people

B

baud rate, 217
Berkeley Mac User Group (BMUG), 159
big screen, 33–35
bookmarks, 27–28
  interactive movies and, 28
  reference products and, 27
books, multimedia, 186

Title	Author	ISBN	Price
INTERNET / COMMUNICATIONS / NETWORKING			12/20/94
CompuServe For Dummies™	by Wallace Wang	1-56884-181-7	$19.95 USA/$26.95 Canada
Modems For Dummies™, 2nd Edition	by Tina Rathbone	1-56884-223-6	$19.99 USA/$26.99 Canada
Modems For Dummies™	by Tina Rathbone	1-56884-001-2	$19.95 USA/$26.95 Canada
MORE Internet For Dummies™	by John R. Levine & Margaret Levine Young	1-56884-164-7	$19.95 USA/$26.95 Canada
NetWare For Dummies™	by Ed Tittel & Deni Connor	1-56884-003-9	$19.95 USA/$26.95 Canada
Networking For Dummies™	by Doug Lowe	1-56884-079-9	$19.95 USA/$26.95 Canada
ProComm Plus 2 For Windows For Dummies™	by Wallace Wang	1-56884-219-8	$19.99 USA/$26.99 Canada
The Internet For Dummies™, 2nd Edition	by John R. Levine & Carol Baroudi	1-56884-222-8	$19.99 USA/$26.99 Canada
The Internet For Macs For Dummies™	by Charles Seiter	1-56884-184-1	$19.95 USA/$26.95 Canada
MACINTOSH			
Macs For Dummies®	by David Pogue	1-56884-173-6	$19.95 USA/$26.95 Canada
Macintosh System 7.5 For Dummies™	by Bob LeVitus	1-56884-197-3	$19.95 USA/$26.95 Canada
MORE Macs For Dummies™	by David Pogue	1-56884-087-X	$19.95 USA/$26.95 Canada
PageMaker 5 For Macs For Dummies™	by Galen Gruman	1-56884-178-7	$19.95 USA/$26.95 Canada
QuarkXPress 3.3 For Dummies™	by Galen Gruman & Barbara Assadi	1-56884-217-1	$19.99 USA/$26.99 Canada
Upgrading and Fixing Macs For Dummies™	by Kearney Rietmann & Frank Higgins	1-56884-189-2	$19.95 USA/$26.95 Canada
MULTIMEDIA			
Multimedia & CD-ROMs For Dummies™, Interactive Multimedia Value Pack	by Andy Rathbone	1-56884-225-2	$29.95 USA/$39.95 Canada
Multimedia & CD-ROMs For Dummies™	by Andy Rathbone	1-56884-089-6	$19.95 USA/$26.95 Canada
OPERATING SYSTEMS / DOS			
MORE DOS For Dummies™	by Dan Gookin	1-56884-046-2	$19.95 USA/$26.95 Canada
S.O.S. For DOS™	by Katherine Murray	1-56884-043-8	$12.95 USA/$16.95 Canada
OS/2 For Dummies™	by Andy Rathbone	1-878058-76-2	$19.95 USA/$26.95 Canada
UNIX			
UNIX For Dummies™	by John R. Levine & Margaret Levine Young	1-878058-58-4	$19.95 USA/$26.95 Canada
WINDOWS			
S.O.S. For Windows™	by Katherine Murray	1-56884-045-4	$12.95 USA/$16.95 Canada
MORE Windows 3.1 For Dummies™, 3rd Edition	by Andy Rathbone	1-56884-240-6	$19.99 USA/$26.99 Canada
PCs / HARDWARE			
Illustrated Computer Dictionary For Dummies™	by Dan Gookin, Wally Wang, & Chris Van Buren	1-56884-004-7	$12.95 USA/$16.95 Canada
Upgrading and Fixing PCs For Dummies™	by Andy Rathbone	1-56884-002-0	$19.95 USA/$26.95 Canada
PRESENTATION / AUTOCAD			
AutoCAD For Dummies™	by Bud Smith	1-56884-191-4	$19.95 USA/$26.95 Canada
PowerPoint 4 For Windows For Dummies™	by Doug Lowe	1-56884-161-2	$16.95 USA/$22.95 Canada
PROGRAMMING			
Borland C++ For Dummies™	by Michael Hyman	1-56884-162-0	$19.95 USA/$26.95 Canada
"Borland's New Language Product" For Dummies™	by Neil Rubenking	1-56884-200-7	$19.95 USA/$26.95 Canada
C For Dummies™	by Dan Gookin	1-878058-78-9	$19.95 USA/$26.95 Canada
C++ For Dummies™	by Stephen R. Davis	1-56884-163-9	$19.95 USA/$26.95 Canada
Mac Programming For Dummies™	by Dan Parks Sydow	1-56884-173-6	$19.95 USA/$26.95 Canada
QBasic Programming For Dummies™	by Douglas Hergert	1-56884-093-4	$19.95 USA/$26.95 Canada
Visual Basic "X" For Dummies™, 2nd Edition	by Wallace Wang	1-56884-230-9	$19.99 USA/$26.99 Canada
Visual Basic 3 For Dummies™	by Wallace Wang	1-56884-076-4	$19.95 USA/$26.95 Canada
SPREADSHEET			
1-2-3 For Dummies™	by Greg Harvey	1-878058-60-6	$16.95 USA/$21.95 Canada
1-2-3 For Windows 5 For Dummies™, 2nd Edition	by John Walkenbach	1-56884-216-3	$16.95 USA/$21.95 Canada
1-2-3 For Windows For Dummies™	by John Walkenbach	1-56884-052-7	$16.95 USA/$21.95 Canada
Excel 5 For Macs For Dummies™	by Greg Harvey	1-56884-186-8	$19.95 USA/$26.95 Canada
Excel For Dummies™, 2nd Edition	by Greg Harvey	1-56884-050-0	$16.95 USA/$21.95 Canada
MORE Excel 5 For Windows For Dummies™	by Greg Harvey	1-56884-207-4	$19.95 USA/$26.95 Canada
Quattro Pro 6 For Windows For Dummies™	by John Walkenbach	1-56884-174-4	$19.95 USA/$26.95 Canada
Quattro Pro For DOS For Dummies™	by John Walkenbach	1-56884-023-3	$16.95 USA/$21.95 Canada
UTILITIES / VCRs & CAMCORDERS			
Norton Utilities 8 For Dummies™	by Beth Slick	1-56884-166-3	$19.95 USA/$26.95 Canada
VCRs & Camcorders For Dummies™	by Andy Rathbone & Gordon McComb	1-56884-229-5	$14.99 USA/$20.99 Canada
WORD PROCESSING			
Ami Pro For Dummies™	by Jim Meade	1-56884-049-7	$19.95 USA/$26.95 Canada
MORE Word For Windows 6 For Dummies™	by Doug Lowe	1-56884-165-5	$19.95 USA/$26.95 Canada
MORE WordPerfect 6 For Windows For Dummies™	by Margaret Levine Young & David C. Kay	1-56884-206-6	$19.95 USA/$26.95 Canada
MORE WordPerfect 6 For DOS For Dummies™	by Wallace Wang, edited by Dan Gookin	1-56884-047-0	$19.95 USA/$26.95 Canada
S.O.S. For WordPerfect™	by Katherine Murray	1-56884-053-5	$12.95 USA/$16.95 Canada
Word 6 For Macs For Dummies™	by Dan Gookin	1-56884-190-6	$19.95 USA/$26.95 Canada
Word For Windows 6 For Dummies™	by Dan Gookin	1-56884-075-6	$16.95 USA/$21.95 Canada
Word For Windows For Dummies™	by Dan Gookin	1-878058-86-X	$16.95 USA/$21.95 Canada
WordPerfect 6 For Dummies™	by Dan Gookin	1-878058-77-0	$16.95 USA/$21.95 Canada
WordPerfect For Dummies™	by Dan Gookin	1-878058-52-5	$16.95 USA/$21.95 Canada
WordPerfect For Windows For Dummies™	by Margaret Levine Young & David C. Kay	1-56884-032-2	$16.95 USA/$21.95 Canada

IDG BOOKS

Order Center: **(800) 762-2974** *(8 a.m.–6 p.m., EST, weekdays)*

Quantity	ISBN	Title	Price	Total

Shipping & Handling Charges

	Description	First book	Each additional book	Total
Domestic	Normal	$4.50	$1.50	$
	Two Day Air	$8.50	$2.50	$
	Overnight	$18.00	$3.00	$
International	Surface	$8.00	$8.00	$
	Airmail	$16.00	$16.00	$
	DHL Air	$17.00	$17.00	$

*For large quantities call for shipping & handling charges.
**Prices are subject to change without notice.

Ship to:

Name _____

Company _____

Address _____

City/State/Zip _____

Daytime Phone _____

Payment: ☐ Check to IDG Books (US Funds Only)

☐ VISA   ☐ MasterCard   ☐ American Express

Card # _____ Expires _____

Signature _____

Subtotal _____

CA residents add
applicable sales tax _____

IN, MA, and MD
residents add
5% sales tax _____

IL residents add
6.25% sales tax _____

RI residents add
7% sales tax _____

TX residents add
8.25% sales tax _____

Shipping _____

Total _____

Please send this order form to:

**IDG Books Worldwide
7260 Shadeland Station, Suite 100
Indianapolis, IN 46256**

*Allow up to 3 weeks for delivery.
Thank you!*

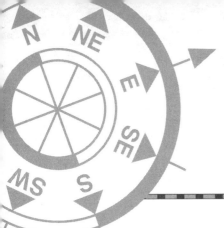

morph

Made popular by Michael Jackson and Peter Gabriel music videos, morphing is an extremely popular special effect that permits any object to transform into another object. Cats turning into dogs, babies into adults, and men into women are but a few of the intriguing morphs seen today. Objects do not need to be similar in order to be morphed. A television can morph into a frog, a car into a teddy bear, and other bizarre transformations are possible with this visually astounding technology.

QuickTime

Developed by Apple, QuickTime is a software product that provides the ability to access sound, video, and animation via computer. Available for Apple Macintosh as well as Microsoft Windows computer systems, QuickTime makes it possible to create and view multimedia content without the need for specialized computer hardware.

real time

You may find, while navigating a multimedia program, that events are a bit sluggish. It may take a few moments for you to go from one place to another, or the glass may take longer than expected to hit the ground when dropped. Many multimedia producers are aware of this disparity between computer and real life. They attempt to provide as realistic an environment as possible by ensuring events in the computer world happen in real time.

MPC (Multimedia Personal Computer)

A standard in the computer industry, defining the equipment necessary for an Intel-based computer system to be considered multimedia capable. The most current version of the standard, MPC Level 2 (MPC2), calls for more computing power than the original specification. MPC and MPC2 are discussed in Appendix A.

on-line

Used to describe any activity taking place on a computer network. Typical examples include on-line banking, on-line shopping, and chatting with friends on-line. Although on-line refers to activity taking place on any computer network, those most commonly used today are the Internet, World Wide Web, and/or commercial on-line services, such as America Online, Prodigy, or CompuServe.

IDG BOOKS WORLDWIDE REGISTRATION CARD

RETURN THIS REGISTRATION CARD FOR FREE CATALOG

Title of this book: Destination MULTIMEDIA

My overall rating of this book: ❑ Very good [1] ❑ Good [2] ❑ Satisfactory [3] ❑ Fair [4] ❑ Poor [5]

How I first heard about this book:

❑ Found in bookstore; name: [6]

❑ Advertisement: [8]

❑ Word of mouth; heard about book from friend, co-worker, etc.: [10]

❑ Book review: [7]

❑ Catalog: [9]

❑ Other: [11]

What I liked most about this book:

What I would change, add, delete, etc., in future editions of this book:

Other comments:

Number of computer books I purchase in a year: ❑ 1 [12] ❑ 2-5 [13] ❑ 6-10 [14] ❑ More than 10 [15]

I would characterize my computer skills as: ❑ Beginner [16] ❑ Intermediate [17] ❑ Advanced [18] ❑ Professional [19]

I use ❑ DOS [20] ❑ Windows [21] ❑ OS/2 [22] ❑ Unix [23] ❑ Macintosh [24] ❑ Other: [25]_____
(please specify)

I would be interested in new books on the following subjects:
(please check all that apply, and use the spaces provided to identify specific software)

❑ Word processing: [26]

❑ Data bases: [28]

❑ File Utilities: [30]

❑ Networking: [32]

❑ Other: [34]

❑ Spreadsheets: [27]

❑ Desktop publishing: [29]

❑ Money management: [31]

❑ Programming languages: [33]

I use a PC at (please check all that apply): ❑ home [35] ❑ work [36] ❑ school [37] ❑ other: [38] _____

The disks I prefer to use are ❑ 5.25 [39] ❑ 3.5 [40] ❑ other: [41]_____

I have a CD ROM: ❑ yes [42] ❑ no [43]

I plan to buy or upgrade computer hardware this year: ❑ yes [44] ❑ no [45]

I plan to buy or upgrade computer software this year: ❑ yes [46] ❑ no [47]

Name: _____ Business title: [48] _____ Type of Business: [49] _____

Address (❑ home [50] ❑ work [51]/Company name: _____)

Street/Suite# _____

City [52]/State [53]/Zipcode [54]: _____ Country [55] _____

❑ **I liked this book!** You may quote me by name in future
IDG Books Worldwide promotional materials.

My daytime phone number is _____

IDG BOOKS

THE WORLD OF
COMPUTER
KNOWLEDGE

❏ # YES!

Please keep me informed about IDG's World of Computer Knowledge.
Send me the latest IDG Books catalog.

COMPUTER
BOOK SERIES
FROM IDG